CREDIT EDUCATION GUIDE

LET'S TALK CREDIT

ATNECIV RODRIGUEZ

MASTER CERTIFIED & LICENSED COACH

The gift you give yourself-
Debt Free & Excellent Credit

First edition 2020
ISBN: 978-1-4583-0140-6
Independently Published

You want to be a home owner? Getting denied credit cards? Do you need to get approved for a car or any loan? Let's Talk Credit is a self-education guide that provides you insight as to what you can do to steer away from debt and starting building positive money habits.

Financial Literacy is one of the most important topics that society is in need of. From the time we are born to the time we pass our world revolves around money. Not only is it important to learn how to make money - it is just as equally important to learn how to keep it. The average american is loaded in debt; in this book, you will learn basic financial concepts to remove debt, learn how to build your credit and start a journey towards financial freedom.

TABLE OF CONTENTS

Credit plays a major role in your overall financial health. Building your credit is a journey that takes time, so it's best to start sooner rather than later. This guide and online tools and tips may help you learn more and answer your questions about credit.

CREDIT BASICS

Credit lets you make purchases by agreeing to repay those funds later. You'll have to apply, and your application could be denied. If your application is approved your credit limit, interest rate, and payment schedule are set by your lender. Having good credit may open the door to a variety of financing options and better rates and terms on your credit accounts.

What's a credit report?
A credit report is a detailed list of your credit history. Its based on informatioln your lenders provide about your credit accounts, your payment history and how you manage each account. In short, your credit history reflects your ability to follow your lenders terms.

What's a credit score?
Your credit score represents how responsible you've been with credit. Think of your credit score as the grade that's given to your credit report by the three national credit reporting agencies- Equifax, Experian, and Transunion. lenders use your credit score to help evaluate your credit risk (or, the likelihoodthat you'll payback the amount you borrowed plus interest.) Generally, the higher your credit score, the lower your risk may be to the lender.

What makes up your credit score?
The credit reporting agencies use various measurements to calculate your credit score. The five key criteria and their impact on your credit score are listed below. (Also see figure on next page)

- **35% Payment History**
- **30% Amounts Owed**
- **15% Length of credit history**
- **10% New credit**
- **10% Credit Mix**

What does a credit score mean?
A good credit score usually makes it easier to qualify for credit. Many lenders have established some standards for credit scores.

Excellent	You generally qualify for the best rates, depneding on your debt to income ratio and collateral value
Good	You typically qualify for credit, depneding on your debt to income ratio and collateral value but may not get best rates
Fair	You may have more difficulty getting credit, and will likely pay higher rates for it.
Poor	You may have difficulty getting unsecured credit.
No credit score	You may not have built up enoug credit to calculate a score, or your credit has been inactive for sometime.

0 +   200 +   400 +   600 +   800 +

WHAT IS A CREDIT SCORE?

Your credit score is a three-digit number generated by a mathematical algorithm using information in your credit report. It's designed to predict risk, specifically, how likely you are to pay your bills.

THE VAST MAJORITY OF PEOPLE WILL HAVE SCORES BETWEEN 600 AND 800.

300
400
500
600
700
850

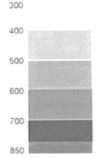

WHAT GOES INTO A CREDIT SCORE?

35%

15%

10%

10%

30%

- ■ Payment History
- ■ Amounts owed
- ■ Length of credit history
- ■ New credit
- ■ Types of credit used

Data from your credit report goes into five major categories that make up a FICO credit score. The scoring model weighs some factors more heavily such as payment history and debt owed.

Personal or demographic information such as age, race, address, marital status, income and employment don't affect the score.

Source: FICO*

myFICO

HOW MUCH DOES A SPECIFIC CHANGE AFFECT A CREDIT SCORE?

	Effect on a 680 score	Effect on a 780 score
Maxed-out card	-10 to -30	-25 to -45
30-day late payment	-60 to -80	-90 to -110
Debt Settlement	-45 to -65	-105 to -125
Bankruptcy	-130 to -150	-220 to -240

Source: FICO*

HISTORY OF CREDIT

Bill Fair and Earl Isaac
In 1956, friends Bill Fair and Earl Isaac established Fair Isaac Corporation to develop and market their credit scoring concept. Initially located in a small apartment in San Rafael, California, Fair Isaac has grown into a NYSE traded company with annual revenues in excess of 600 million dollars. Their credit scoring model is known as FICO.

The Number that Changed the World
In the early years, Fair Isaac marketed their scoring system to financial service companies seeking to make faster and more accurate credit decisions. In 1989, as businesses were discovering the power of computerization, Fair Isaac introduced an automated credit scoring software package that was quickly embraced by credit card issuers. But the big catalyst for the near universal acceptance of credit scoring came in 1995 when mortgage giants Fannie Mae and Freddie Mac stipulated that mortgage lenders incorporate FICO scores in their approval process. The rest is history.

Life, Credit Repair, and FICO
There are other credit scores, and most are hopeful of making market inroads; some, like the Vantage Score, are contenders. For now, the clear leader and the one that matters to your credit repair effort, is the FICO score. It is a practical reality; lenders, with few exceptions, use FICO. And when it comes to our credit repair program, everything from the dispute letters we write to the credit management suggestions we make to our clients revolve around the mechanics of FICO.

DEBT-TO-INCOME (DTI) RATIO

What is debt- to- income (DTI) ratio?
DTI ratio shows how much of your income goes toward paying your current debt obligations/ Basically, it compares how much your owe each month to how much your earn.

Your DTI is based on your before-tax income, and current debt obligations may include such things as your monthly mortgage (or rent), credit card, and other credit account payments, and alimony or child support. Lenders may use your DTI to assess your ability to pay back debt. A low DTI is a good indicator that you have enough income to meet your monthly obligations, take care of additional or unexpected expenses, and make the additional payment each month on the new credit account.

When you apply for credit, your lender may calculate your DTI ratio based on verified income and debt amounts, and the result may differ from the one shown here. You do not need to list alimony, child support, or separate maintenance income unless you want it considered when calculating your result. If you receive income that is nontaxable, it may be upwardly adjusted to account for the nontaxable status.

DTI Example
Based on $5000 monthly income, with $1,500 in monthly debt payment.

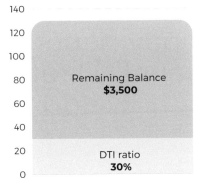

Remaining Balance **$3,500**

DTI ratio **30%**

What does DTI mean?
A lower DTI may make it easier to qualify for new credit. Some lenders have established standards for DTI ratios.

Looking good **35%-or less**	Relative to your income, your debt is at a manageable level. You most likely have money left over for saving or spending after you've paid your bills. Lenders generally view a lower DTI as favorable
Opportunity to improve **36%-49%**	You may want to consider lowering your DTI to get into a better position to handle potential financial emergencies. If you're looking to borrow, keep in mind that lenders use different factors to determine your ability to repay, including your monthly income and financial obligations like loan payments, rent and bills.
Consider taking action **50% or more**	With more than half your income going toward debt payments, you may not have much money left to save, spend, or handle unforeseen expenses. With this DTI ratio, lenders may limit your borrowing options.

TIP:

Before taking on any new debt, estimate the monthly payments and re-estimate your DTI ratio so you can see how additional debt may change it.

THE 5 C'S OF CREDIT

What do lenders look for?

Lenders look at a number of things to evaluate your credit application, which may include the 5c's of Credit. While the definitions and use of the 5 C's may vary between lenders, it's a good idea to understand the basic concepts. This way, you'll know where you stand and may be ina a better position to provide as much helpful detail as possible when you apply.

1. **Credit History-** Your track record of managing credit and making payments over time. The way you've handled credit obligations in the past helps indicate what a lender may expenct in the future.
2. **Capacity-** Your ability to comfortably mange your payments. Lenders looks at your debt-to-income (DTI) ratio when they're evaluating your credit application to assess whether you're able to take on a new debt.
3. **Collaterral -** Something you own that you may pledge to secure a loan. Collateral is important to lenders because it offsets the risk they take when they offer you credit. USing your assets as collateral gives you more borrowing options, including credit accounts that may have lower interest rates and better terms.
4. **Capital-** Savings, investments, and other assets that you could use to repay a loan if you experience a financial setback. Capital matters because the more of it you have, the more financially secure you are, and the more confident the lender may be about extending your credit.
5. **Conditions-** The economic environment and how yu polan to use the funds. Lenders are interested in conditions, because they may impact your financial situation and ability to repay the loan.

MISTAKES ON CREDIT FILE

Mixed credit reports are caused when the credit bureau places information belonging to another consumer on your credit report. If you've got a common name, there's a chance that your credit report could be crossed with another consumer with the same name. Since the credit scoring software is not able to distinguish between your credit data and credit data belonging to another person, it will "score" the information even if it's incorrect. Consequently, if the other consumer with the same name has poor credit, this information will now appear on your credit file resulting in a possible denial of credit.

The reason mixed files are so hard to correct is because the lender typically is not sending in incorrect information. The problem is being caused by the credit bureau inadvertently co-mingling data belonging to two consumers and placing it on one credit report. So, the lender cannot fix the problem because they're not causing it. Additionally, the credit reporting agencies are under no obligation to proactively investigate the information on your credit reports to determine if it's yours or if it belongs to another person with the same name. You have to pull your own credit reports, review the information and then file a formal dispute with the credit bureaus if you find data that you believe is incorrect or belongs to someone else.

According to myfico.com, additional reasons for incorrect data in credit files include:
- The person applied for credit under different versions of their name (Robert Jones, Bob Jones, etc.).
- Someone made a clerical error in reading or entering name or address information from a hand-written application.
- The person gave an inaccurate Social Security number, or the number was misread by the lender.
- Sr.'s and Jr.'s living within the same household get account information crossed.
- Loan or credit card payments were inadvertently applied to the wrong account.

ITEMS TO LOOK FOR

When reviewing your file

- This account does not belong to me.
- This is a duplicate account.
- I never authorized this account.
- The balance on this account is incorrect.
- There is no past due balance on this account.
- This account is closed with a $0 balance and has a positive payment history.
- You are not reporting the correct limit on my account.
- This account was included in a bankruptcy and should have a $0 balance/
- I was not 30, 60, 90 or 120 days late on this account.
- This account was paid.
- This account was closed by me, not the creditor.
- The open date on this account is incorrect.
- This account is still open.
- I am only an authorized user on this account. Please remove it.
- You are reporting my home equity line of credit as a revolving account.
- I never authorized this inquiry.
- This public record has been satisfied/released/dismissed/vacated.
- You are listing the wrong file/released/satisfied date on this public record.
- The date of last activity on this account is incorrect.
- This account never went into foreclosure/repossession.
- The 7-year reporting period has expired on this account.
- The statute of limitations on this account expired.
- You cannot report it or re-insert it.
- You are reporting someone else's information on my credit report that has the same name that I do.
- You are reporting the wrong social security number, birth date, spouse's name, phone number on my credit report.
- You are reporting wrong/expired/misspelled addresses on my credit report.
- You are reporting misspelled/wrong names on my credit report.
- You are reporting outdated/wrong employment information on my credit report.
- This student loan account has been deferred.

VANTAGE SCORE V FICO SCORE

Since the 1970s, credit scores have played an increasingly vital role in the lending industry. Fair Isaac and Company began assigning credit scores to consumers based upon various factors over 40 years ago, and these scores are now reviewed not only by prospective lenders, but also by landlords, insurers and governmental agencies. But the computation process for the FICO score has some limitations; for example, a consumer has to have a credit line open for at least six months before it will show up on a FICO credit report. This and other deficiencies have led the three major bureaus to establish a new credit score model known as Vantage Score, which evaluates customers according to a somewhat different set of criteria that can be much more forgiving in some instances.

A Collaborative Effort

The three major credit bureaus have used the FICO scoring model for decades, but the differences in how each agency computes its scores has led to numerous discrepancies that are often problematic for both lenders and consumers. The VantageScore model is designed to provide a much more standardized grading system than the one used by Fair Isaac and Company. The first version of Vantage appeared in 2006, followed by Vantage 2.0 in 2010, which was modified in response to the changes that swept over the lending industry after the Subprime Mortgage Meltdown of 2008.

The VantageScore Model Methodology

VantageScore credit scores are computed in a fundamentally different manner than FICO scores. They start with a somewhat different set of criteria than FICO and also assign a different weighting to each segment. A comparison of the two is shown as follows:

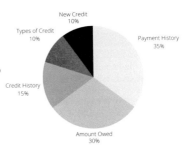

FICO
- The Consumer's Payment History: 35%
- Total Amounts Owed by the Consumer: 30%
- Length of the Consumer's Credit History: 15%
- Types of Credit Used by the Consumer: 10%
- Amount of the Consumer's New Credit: 10%

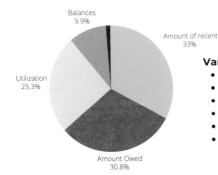

VantageScore
- Amount of the Consumer's Recent Credit: 30%
- The Consumer's Payment History: 28%
- Utilization of the Consumer's Current Credit: 23%
- Size of the Consumer's Account Balances: 9%
- Depth of the Consumer's Credit: 9%
- Amount of the Consumer's Available Credit: 1%

The VantageScore model is also quantified differently than FICO scores. It still uses a numerical range for its scores, but it also assigns a corresponding letter grade for a given range, in some instances, that helps consumers to understand the quality of their score. The grade is statistically based upon the ratio of consumers who are likely to charge off versus those who will pay on time. The VantageScore system is broken down as follows:

- 901 to 990 = A – 1 charge off for every 300 consumers who pay on time
- 801 to 900 = B – 1 charge off for every 50 consumers who pay on time
- 701 to 800 = C – 1 charge off for every 10 consumers who pay on time
- 601 to 700 = D – 1 charge off for every 5 consumers who pay on time
- 501 to 600 = F – 1 charge off for every 1 consumers who pay on time

As with FICO, the consumer's creditworthiness matches his or her score and grade. Each of the three major credit bureaus computes a score based on the VantageScore model using its own data. Of course, while all three bureaus use the exact same model to compute the VantageScore credit score, it can still differ from one bureau to another because each bureau typically records slightly different information in their consumer files.

The VantageScore Benefit
One of the chief advantages that the VantageScore model brings is the ability to provide a score to a large segment of consumers (about 30 to 35 million) who are currently unscorable when traditional methodologies are applied. The VantageScore model differs from FICO in that a line of credit only has to be open for a single month in order to be factored in, yet this model takes 24 months of consumer credit activity into account, whereas FICO only looks back for six months. The longer look back period can be a big help for consumers who are working to rebuild their credit and are able to show a marked improvement over the longer time span. The VantageScore credit score is also designed to serve as a "predictive score" for those with thin credit histories by indicating the probability that they will meet their future payment obligations in a timely manner. It can also use rent and utility payments in its computations if they are reported by the landlord and/or utility provider.

VantageScore 3.0
The most recent version of the VantageScore model represents a substantial improvement over the previous two models. It was created beginning with over 900 data points from 45 million consumer credit files spanning two overlapping time frames from 2009 to 2012. However, it only uses about half the number of reason codes (which signify various reasons why the consumer's credit score carries the number that it has been assigned), and these codes have been rewritten in plain language that consumers can easily understand. VantageScore Solutions, the company behind the model, also provides an online resource where consumers can look up their reason codes, which can be found at www.reasoncode.org.As mentioned previously, the risk assessment formula that is used in the model is now identical for each of the major bureaus because it employs uniform definitions for consumer payment and credit information that is received by each bureau. The VantageScore model also claims that the predictive score in this version will be 25% more accurate than the previous one due to the substantial increase in both the quality and quantity of data upon which the model is based.

Impact with Lenders
Despite the hype with which the three credit bureaus have promoted their new scoring system, it has been slow to catch on in the lending industry. The VantageScore model remains a very distant second to the traditional FICO score in the amount of market share that it has carved out among lenders. As of April 2012, less than 6% of the credit scoring market and only 10% of the major banks use the VantageScore model in their underwriting.

The Bottom Line
Although its method of computation is considered to be more fair and realistic than the FICO model, it will likely take some time for lenders to become comfortable with shifting to this alternative methodology. Nevertheless, the number of institutions that accept the VantageScore model is growing, and its popularity will likely continue to increase with its ability to tap a new market of potential lending customers.

MAKING A LOT OF MONEY WILL HELP YOUR CREDIT REPORT AND YOUR CREDIT SCORES.
The fact of the matter is that your salary has nothing to do with your credit reports or credit scores. Your salary is important to lenders but not important in a credit worthiness way. It's important for them to know that you have the ability to make the payments for the next 5, 10 or 30 years. One is as important as the other but you won't be approved for the best interest rates if your credit is poor, regardless of how much money you make.

A GREAT CREDIT SCORE IS A RESULT OF A CREDIT REPORT WITHOUT ANY LATE PAYMENTS.
Paying all of your bills on time is a great start. And, you will not have excellent credit reports and scores without a clean payment history. But, it's not the only thing. A full 2/3 of your credit score is derived from things other than how well you pay your bills. Keeping your credit usage ratio to less than 30% of your balance keeps positive recording items on your credit report. In addition, having a mixture of credit that includes a mortgage, car payment and 2 credit cards that are paid timely will increase your credit score.

ALL THREE OF YOUR CREDIT REPORTS AND CREDIT SCORES WILL BE THE SAME.
The opposite is what is correct. It's a certainty that all three of your credit reports will be different and, therefore, so will all three of your credit scores. There are three primary reasons why this is true:

- Not all of your accounts will be reported to all three credit -reporting agencies. Since reporting is a voluntary act, not all lenders report to all three.
- You will most certainly have a different number of inquiries on your three credit reports. Since most lenders just pull one of your three credit reports, you will have a different number of inquiries on your reports.
- Lenders don't always update their accounts on your credit reports at the same time. Because of this, your reports will be different.

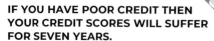

IF YOU HAVE POOR CREDIT THEN YOUR CREDIT SCORES WILL SUFFER FOR SEVEN YEARS.

This is not true. Credit scores are dynamic, meaning they are constantly changing. This means that the scores are calculated based on your credit information at that time. If the information on your credit files changes tomorrow, then so will your scores.

DEBIT CARDS CAN HELP YOUR CREDIT REPORTS AND SCORES.

This isn't true. Debit Cards are nothing more than plastic access to your checking account. The confusion comes in part because of the Visa or MasterCard logos that are on the debit card. They look exactly like credit cards so the assumption is that they count. If you become overdrawn on your checking account because you don't track the use of your check card then it could result in bounced checks.

PAYING OFF (OR "SETTLING") LATE PAYMENTS, TAX LIENS, COLLECTIONS OR JUDGMENTS WILL REMOVE THEM FROM YOUR CREDIT REPORTS.

It's not that easy. While it's the responsible and right thing to do, don't expect any miracles to occur just because you pay off some or all of your negative credit related debts. After late payments or other derogatory items have been paid and settled they will be updated on your credit reports to show "paid collection" or "released tax lien" or "satisfied judgment", which is much better than the alternative but they may still be there negatively impacting your credit scores.

CREDIT MYTHS

CANCELING CREDIT CARDS BOOSTS MY SCORE
Most experts agree that most creditors want to see at least two or three pieces of active credit to prove you can manage debt responsibly. Making sure that at all time your credit report is showing credit that is available that is greater than 70% of the available limit is where you want to be. Making sure that creditors and potential lenders see that you are managing your debt correctly is key.

CREDIT SCORES ARE LOCKED IN FOR SIX MONTHS
Fair Isaac Corp.'s models are dynamic, meaning that your credit score changes as soon as data on your credit report change. When a score is calculated, for all intents and purposes it then goes away and is recalculated the next time someone pulls your file.

I DON'T NEED TO CHECK MY CREDIT REPORT IF I PAY MY BILLS ON TIME
According to the Consumer Federation of America and the National Credit Reporting Association, they have found that 78 percent of those analyzed had credit files that were missing a revolving account in good standing, while 33 percent of files lacked a mortgage account that had never been late. Twenty-nine percent contained conflicting information on how many times the consumer had been 60 days late on payments. It's been calculated that 80 percent of all credit reports have erroneous information ranging from a wrong birth date to accounts you never applied for.

HOW MUCH IS SCORE IMPACTED BY NEGATIVE ACCOUNTS

It has always been a trade secret – how much does a new late payment or collection hurt my credit score? Recently, the developers of the FICO scoring system have offered some insight into this previously guarded information. The answer can be found by focusing on three different consumers with starting scores of 680, 720 and 780. (FICO scores range from 300-850) The FICO study then estimated the impact on the score based on a variety of negative events with a mortgage loan, such as a 30-day late payment, short sale, foreclosure, bankruptcy, etc.

FICO Score Impact Findings:
- The impact on the FICO score (drop in points) is greater when the starting score is higher. For example, a foreclosure would drop a starting score of 680 anywhere from 85 to 105 points, compared to 140 to 160 points if the starting score was a 780. This makes sense because the 680 score already reflects some degree of risky behavior (thus the starting score of 680 vs. 780)—so the point impact isn't as great.
- There is little difference in score impact between a short sale, deed-in-lieu, settlement or foreclosure. A bankruptcy has the most substantial impact on the FICO score—with the potential to drop a 780 score by 240 points (to 540).

The study also provides insight into how long it takes the score to fully recover from these negative postings. Credit scores are "forgiving"—as negative information ages, it has less impact on the score as long as current credit behaviors are positive.

FICO Score Recovery Findings:
- Full recovery to the starting FICO score (prior to the posting of the negative item) is faster when the starting score is lower and the negative item posted was less severe. For example, it takes a short 9 months to get back to 680 when the negative item posted on the mortgage was a 30-day late. This is compared to the 7 to 10 years to get back to a score of 780 if a bankruptcy was posted.
- *For a score to fully recover from a short sale, deed in lieu, settlement or foreclosure takes 3 years for a 680 starting score, 7 years for a 720 starting score and 7 years for a 780 starting score.

** It is important to keep in mind that the negative impact on the credit score can be offset by credit building techniques such as keeping all future payments on time, responsible and consistent use of a variety of credit and keeping balances low.

The study is welcome information because for the first time, FICO provides us with an inside look at the direct impacts and point losses on the score. This information can help consumers get a better sense of how various negative indicators on a mortgage loan could impact their FICO score—and how long it can take for their score to fully recover. It's important to note these findings are basic guidelines and the exact impact on your score will be unique to your individual situation.

6 WORST ITEMS THAT APPEAR ON CREDIT FILE

It's easy to make a mistake or experience hardship when it comes to paying your bills. Some mistakes are so detrimental; you want to avoid them at all cost. Since future creditors and lenders use your credit report to make decisions about you, it's important to understand how each of these impact your credit file.

Charge-offs

Missing your payments for 6 months or more could cause your creditors to deem your account as uncollectible. When this happens, the creditors write that debt off as a loss against their income taxes. Charged-off accounts are allowed to be reported on your credit report for seven years. Just because a debt is charged off (or written off) does not mean the debt is forgiven, the money is still owed. The creditor will usually sell or assign the debt to a collection agency or a lawyer for collection.

Some companies will continue to charge interest, but most don't. If they do decide to keep charging interest, they have to continue to report it as income, most companies would rather just write it off and be done with it.

Having charge offs on your credit report usually results in the consumer being denied credit by other lenders. Even worse, it can also affect the interest rate that other lenders charge on current debts even if those lenders were not impacted by the charge off themeselves.

If you find yourself late on your payments, you should always try to contact the lender and let them know you are having problems meeting your financial obligations. Ignoring the situation and letting it get to charge off status always makes it worse. You can usually avoid your account being charged off by at least letting them know you intend to pay and by making small payments as often as you can.

It's much easier to get a paid charge off removed from your credit report than it is an unpaid charge off. When you dispute the charge off with the credit bureaus, they have 30 days to verify to account with the creditor. If the account is paid, many times the creditor will just ignore the verification request.

6 WORST ITEMS THAT APPEAR ON CREDIT FILE

Collections

Not only will creditors charge off your account after a period of non-payments, they may also hire a third-party debt collector to collect payment from you. Your credit report may or may not be updated to reflect a collection status.

Bankruptcy

Filing bankruptcy allows you to legally remove liability for some or all of your debts, depending on the type of bankruptcy you file. Your credit report will reflect each of the accounts you included in your bankruptcy. Even though the bankruptcy information can legally remain on your credit report for seven to 10 years, you can begin rebuilding your credit soon after your debt have been discharged.

Foreclosure

If you default on your mortgage loan, your lender will repossess your home and auction it off to recover the amount of the mortgage. This process is known as foreclosure. When your home is foreclosed it can severely damage your credit, limiting your ability to obtain new credit in the future. A foreclosure can remain on your credit report for seven years.

Tax liens

When you don't pay property taxes on your home or another piece of property, the government can seize the property and auction it off for the unpaid taxes. Unpaid tax liens can remain on your credit report for 15 years, while paid tax liens remain for 10.

Lawsuits or judgments

Some creditors may take you to court and sue you for a debt, in the event other collection efforts fail. If a judgment is entered against you, it can remain on your credit report for 7 years from the date of filing, even after you satisfy the judgment.

ESTABLISHING CREDIT

You may establish credit by credit products responsibly, paying back what you've borrowed in a timely fashion, and making your monthly payments according to your credit agreement.

Lay the foundation for good credit

Activities that dont directly impact your credit report may still be used to demonstrate your financial responsibility.
- Pay your utility, cell phone or other bills on time every time.
- Open a check account and use your your debit card responsibly.
- Build a savings account.

Ways to get started

- Consider gasoline, secured cards, and retail cards. They might be easier to acquire than bank-issued credit cards. Be aware that they may have different terms than other credit cards, so make sure to review them carefully and make your payments on time.

- Become and authorized user on a trusted person's credit card. Keep in mind that not all lenders report authorized user accounts to the credit bureaus, so make sure to find out tha t your credit company does.

- Apply for a loan with a co-borrower or co-signer. Remember that your co-signer or co-applicant also takes responsibility for payment. That means the credit history will be reflected on both of your credit reports.

- Charge only what you can afford.

- Avoid maxing out your credit accounts. Its generally a good idea to keep your balances under 30% of your credit limit.

How long will it take?

Each person's situation is different, so it's hard to say how long it will take for you to build your credit. Instead, think of it as an ongoing process. Keep working toward making your credit the best it can be.

IMPROVING YOUR CREDIT

Improving your credit score may open doors to a stronger financial future. Heres what you may do to raise your score.

Check your credit report

You may request a free copy of your credit report from each of the three major credit reporting agencies- Equifax, Experian, and Transunikon - once a year at **AnnualCreditReport.com** or call toll-free 1-877-322-8228. If you find information you believe doesn't belong to you or is inaccurate, contact the businesses that issued the account or the credit reporting company that issued the report. Checking your own credit won't affect your score.

Tip: Staggering your individual request may help you track your credit history over the year.

Be responsible

Consistent on-time payments show lenders that you're responsible about paying back what you borrow. Your payment history makes up 35% of your credit score. If you've missed a payment, pay as soon as possible-it makes a difference.

Tip: Sign up for automatic bill pay.

Be consistent

Practice healthy credit habits, like making all of your payments on time, paying more than the minimum, and keeping your balances low.

Tip: Keep your long-standing accounts open. The length of your credit history and available credit both factor into your credit score.

Keep your balances low

Generally, avoid carrying a balance that's more than 30% of your credit limit. Also, pay more than the minimum each month whenever possible.

Tip: Building good credit depends on your ability to pay back what you borrow. Start small with what you can comfortably pay each month along with your other obligations.

Stabilize your situation

If you're working toward rebuilding your credit, set a budget and make at least minimum payments on time for each account.

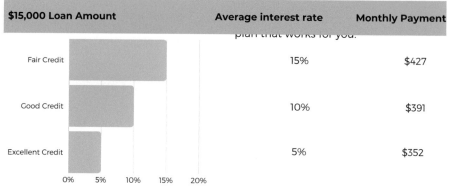

$15,000 Loan Amount	Average interest rate	Monthly Payment
Fair Credit	15%	$427
Good Credit	10%	$391
Excellent Credit	5%	$352

Sample Monthly payments based on credit score   Scenarios are hypothetical- Illustration only

MAINTAINING GOOD CREDIT

If you are new to using credit, or are re-establishing a damaged credit, utilize these tips to keep you good credit on track.

Setting up on-line payments for your bills is any easy, secure and convenient way to simplify your finances. Automatic payments will make sure your bills are paid on time and will prevent you from incurring any future late fees.

Charge small amounts regularly on each card -- but not more than you can pay off each month.

Use your credit wisely. Do not open unnecessary credit accounts. The extra 10% off you save to open a department store credit account may be quickly offset by the possible decrease in your credit score because (1) you may spend more, and (2) you are adding an additional trade account and additional inquiry to your credit file. Also, before you apply for additional credit, make sure your rent, mortgage and car payments can be easily met. If not, do not apply for additional credit until your income and debt are under control.

Be cautious with credit card solicitations. Just because you receive one of these offers does not mean that you can afford the additional credit. Many companies are soliciting consumers who based on their past spending histories will charge big balances at high interest rates.
Do not close credit accounts unless it is absolutely necessary in order to close a loan. When you delete a trade line you also delete the corresponding credit history and may inadvertently lower your credit score.

It is always better to pay off credit cards before an auto or mortgage loan to get the biggest score increases.

Review your credit file at least twice a year, correct any errors and omissions.

MANAGING YOUR CREDIT

Repaying your debt may sometimes feel challenging. That's why making a planto manage your payments and balances may help. Take a look at these tips and discover some small steps you may take today to make managing your debt easier.

Consider debt consolidation

Transferring multiple debts, especially those with higher interest rates, intoa single new loan may help simplify the repayment process and lead to a lower rate that migt reduce your monthly payments. *

Pay off debt faster

Refinancing your debt to a shorter term may help you pay it off faster and reduce yout total borrowing cots. Be advised that shortening your term could increase your monthly payments.

Lower your monthly payments to help free up cash

Contact your lenders about potentially refinancing at a lowr interest rate or extending the terms of your loans. Keep in mind that extending the term of your loan may lower your monthly payments, but you may pay more in interest over the life of the loan.

Pay off your most expensive loan first

Pay off the debt with the highest interest rate first to reduce your overall interest costs.

Know your limits

Being close to or maxing out your credit cards may negatively impact your credit score. It's generally a good idea to keep your balances under 30% of your credit limit.

Sample Monthly payments based on based on length of loan   Scenarios are hypothetical- Illustration only

$15,000 Loan Amount at 7.5% interest	Interest paid	Total Paid
10 Years — $180 monthly payment	$6,602	$21,602
5 Years — $302 monthly payment	$3,141	$18,141
3 Years — $462 monthly payment	$1,860	$16,860

$0 $1,000 $2,000 $3,000 $4,000 $5,000 $6,000 $7,000

USING PRE-PAID CREDIT CARDS

Prepaid Cards

There are no credit requirements to obtain one of these cards, because you are not borrowing money.

These cards can be convenient for parents to use with children, because they can put a specific amount on the card for their child to use.

Cash or Credit

Prepaid cards don't require a credit check or proof of income (which will soon be required under new federal credit card laws), another selling point for young adults, part-time workers or others with credit problems.

Carrying a card is safer than carrying around large amounts of cash.

Kids & Money

Buyers are also finding creative uses for the prepaid cards, giving them as gifts or using them for the kids' allowance.

Prepaid cards are becoming popular among consumers, gift givers, employers, and even the Social Security Administration. Similar to gift cards at specific retailers, prepaid cards allow individuals to load the cards with a specific amount of money and use them for purchases. However, unlike store gift cards, prepaid cards typically display the logo of one of the major credit card companies (Visa, American Express, MasterCard, Discover) and allow the user to make purchases anywhere that the credit card company is accepted. Generally, the individual can spend only the amount that they "prepaid" on the card, but they can add more money, or "reload" the card at any time.

Because you cannot accumulate debt, prepaid debit cards can be extremely helpful when managing a tight budget. There is a finite amount of money you can spend, which is the amount of money deposited onto your card. There are several ways you can add money to your prepaid debit card by transferring funds onto it, however it is important to note that you may incur additional fees when you use your card. These fees include an initial payment to acquire the card, a monthly usage fee, and in most cases, a transaction fee any time you want to add money to the balance on the card.

Prepaid cards offer the convenience of a credit card, such as paying at the pump or shopping online. Carrying a card is safer than carrying around large amounts of cash. Prepaid cards don't require a credit check or proof of income (which will soon be required under new federal credit card laws), another selling point for young adults, part-time workers or others with credit problems. Buyers are also finding creative uses for the prepaid cards, giving them as gifts or using them for the kids' allowance.

Some service providers, such as hotels and car rental agencies, don't accept prepaid cards. If they do, they usually put a temporary hold on the card until the transaction is settled. That could tie up the funds on the card and prevent you from using it somewhere else in the meantime.

DEBIT CARD MANAGEMENT

1

When you understand how to manage your finances, you've got an invaluable tool in taking control of your life. Wise use of these skills can provide peace of mind, financial freedom, increased buying power and a secure future.

2

In recent years debit cards have risen in popularity, usually replacing payment by cash and check. A debit card, unlike a credit card, is tied directly to a checking account. When you make a purchase with a credit card, you are borrowing money from the card issuer, where a debit card purchase withdraws money directly from your bank account.

3

Each method has its own benefits. Credit card users who pay off their bill each month benefit from a free loan of money. On the other hand, consumers concerned with debt load can limit their spending by using debit cards. Because your debit card is tied to your bank account, consider the following precautions when you use it:

WHEN USING A DEBIT CARD DON'T FORGET TO:

- Keep sales receipts or copies.
- Record your transactions in your check register as soon as possible or check transactions online.
- Remember to account for any bank fees that may apply.
- Review statements carefully. If you suspect a mistake, call your financial institution immediately.

STOP SURCHARGES

For maximum security, take advantage of free alerts for your debit card. Some financial institutions offer automatic account alerts by phone and email, such as when:
- ATM withdrawals or any debit card activity exceeds your set dollar limits
- Your online ID or passwords change
- Large transactions are made

SECURITY

Many banks charge a fee if you use another institution's ATM with your debit card, and they usually charge non-account holders to use their ATMs. Instead of paying extra, choose a bank or credit union with ATMs convenient to where you live and work or use your debit card to get cash back when making purchases.

KEEP YOUR PIN SECURE

Your debit card will require a (PIN) for security. Choose a unique number. Avoid obvious choices like your address, phone number or birth date. Always keep your PIN private, memorize it, don't write it down anywhere and never tell it to anyone. If you feel your PIN has been compromised, change your number immediately by contacting your financial institution.

EXTRA PRECAUTIONS

1
ZERO LIABILITY
This generally means you're not liable for unauthorized purchases made on your debit cards as long as you notify your financial institution immediately. Check with your financial institution to make sure Zero Liability applies to your card.

2
FUNDS AND FRAUD
Federal law mandates that financial institutions replace funds for losses resulting from fraudulent card use within ten business days of notification. However, in many cases, you'll have access to funds within five business days of notification– sometimes sooner.

3
THE RIGHT TO DISPUTE
You may have dispute resolution options should an issue arise with a debit card purchase. This often applies to signed purchases only. Check with your card issuer, and save all of your receipts.

KNOW YOUR LIMITS

Many debit cards have daily spending and cash withdrawal limits. These limits are meant to protect you in case your card is stolen. But remember, your card might be declined if you exceed your limits even if you have enough money in the bank. Know your limits and contact your lender if you need to raise or lower amounts.

KEEP TRACK OF YOUR SPENDING

Also remember to track your spending. When you make a purchase, withdraw money from your account or pay bills that exceed your account balance, you may be subject to "overdraft fees." Some financial institutions offer overdraft protection, and they'll cover your check or debit transaction so it doesn't bounce. But this protection often comes with a price tag too. You may be charged a fee for each purchase that uses overdraft, as well as an additional fee for being overdrawn. Balance your account regularly to avoid added fees. Information adapted from Visa.

CHOOSE AND USE CARDS WISELY

If you're like most consumers, you may be dependent on credit cards. That's understandable because they offer convenience, enable you to take advantage of opportunities, and can get you through emergencies. Establishing credit is also a must if you plan to ever borrow money to buy a car or home. However, credit can also get you into trouble. At best, credit cards can make it difficult to stick to a budget. At worst, they can tempt you to overspend to the point of not being able to pay your bills. To enjoy the benefits of credit and avoid the potential pitfalls, you need to understand the basics of getting, using and managing a credit card.

Credit cards allow you to buy things and pay for them over time. But remember, buying with credit is a loan — you have to pay the money back. And some issuers charge an annual fee for their cards. Some credit card issuers also provide "courtesy" checks to their customers. You can use these checks in place of your card, but they're not a gift — they're also a loan that you must pay back. And if you don't pay your bill on time or in full when it's due, you will owe a finance charge — the dollar amount you pay to use credit. The finance charge depends in part on your outstanding balance and the annual percentage rate (APR).

Do You Want a Credit Card or a Charge Card?

With a traditional "credit" card, you charge items on your account and receive a bill later, which you have the option to pay in full or in part (at least as much as the "minimum payment due"). If you don't pay the account in full, the remaining balance will carry over to the next month and you'll be charged interest on it. This is referred to as revolving credit.

The other type of card, often referred to as a "charge" card, doesn't allow you to carry a balance from month to month; you have to pay off the total balance when you get your bill. These cards offer the convenience of plastic without the danger of getting into debt or paying high interest charges. American Express is a good example of this type of card.

Both kinds of cards are offered under a variety of labels (gold, platinum, premier, and the like), each one offering different features and benefits. The gold and platinum types of cards are typically offered to consumers who have an excellent credit history.

The Fine Print

When applying for credit cards, it's important to shop around. Fees, interest rates, finance charges, and benefits can vary greatly. And, in some cases, credit cards might seem like great deals until you read the fine print and disclosures. When you're trying to find the credit card that's right for you, look at the:

Annual percentage rate (APR) — The APR is a measure of the cost of credit, expressed as a yearly interest rate. It must be disclosed before your account can be activated, and it must appear on your account statements. The card issuer also must disclose the "periodic rate" — the rate applied to your outstanding balance to figure the finance charge for each billing period.

Some credit card plans allow the issuer to change your APR when interest rates or other economic indicators — called indexes — change. Because the rate change is linked to the index's performance, these plans are called "variable rate" programs. Rate changes raise or lower the finance charge on your account. If you're considering a variable rate card, the issuer also must tell you that the rate may change and how the rate is determined.

Before you become obligated on the account, you also must receive information about any limits on how much and how often your rate may change.

Grace period

—The grace period is the number of days you have to pay your bill in full without triggering a finance charge. For example, the credit card company may say that you have 25 days from the statement date, provided you paid your previous balance in full by the due date. The statement date is on the bill.

The grace period usually applies only to new purchases. Most credit cards do not give a grace period for cash advances and balance transfers. Instead, interest charges start right away. If your card includes a grace period, the issuer must mail your bill at least 14 days before the due date so you'll have enough time to pay.

Annual fees —

Many issuers charge annual membership or participation fees.

Some card issuers assess the fee in monthly installments.

Transaction fees and other charges

—Some issuers charge a fee if you use the card to get a cash advance, make a late payment, or exceed your credit limit.

Some charge a monthly fee if you use the card — or if you don't.

Customer service —Customer service is something most people don't consider, or appreciate, until there's a problem. Look for a 24-hour toll-free telephone number.

Unauthorized charges

—If your card is used without your permission, you can be held responsible for up to $50 per card. If you report the loss before the card is used, you can't be held responsible for any unauthorized charges. To minimize your liability, report the loss as soon as possible. Some issuers have 24-hour toll-free telephone numbers to accept emergency information. It's a good idea to follow-up with a letter to the issuer — include your account number, the date you noticed your card missing, and the date you reported the loss. Keep a record — in a safe place separate from your cards — of your account numbers, expiration dates, and the telephone numbers of each card issuer so you can report a loss quickly. (Information courtesy of the FTC)

CREDIT VS DEBIT: WHICH SHOULD YOU CHOOSE?

Since credit and debit payments account for the majority of consumer in-store purchasing in the United States – is one considered a better option than the other? The debate over which is better to use – credit versus debit – has been ongoing. However, research indicates that since 2000, the number of debit transactions has more than doubled, while the number of credit card transactions has fallen by nearly half. Does this mean that debit is a better choice? Consider the comparison below.

Credit Cards

Credit cards are convenient and easy to use often allowing consumers to purchase goods and services they would otherwise not be able to afford. Credit is money a creditor makes available to a person to borrow with the option of future repayment. In exchange for the credit, the lender is paid back the original money plus any interest usually paid on a monthly basis.

Debit Cards

Debit cards are normally associated with or linked to an individual's regular checking or savings account at their local bank. As a purchase is made, money is electronically withdrawn from the account linked to the debit card. Note: Even though a debit card may have a Visa or MasterCard insignia logo on it, it is not reported on your credit report as a charge card.

Depending on what you are buying, what type of purchase it is, and how much money you have, it may be more beneficial to use credit. As long as you not over extending yourself and routinely pay off the balance, it may be wise to use credit if:

You are making a major purchase.

Credit cards offer the strongest protection on purchase disputes. Whereas, when a purchase is made with a debit card, the money is gone from your account. In cases where you are spending a large amount or the purchase is made online, credit may be the better payment option. You may also get increased warranty protection and insurance against theft of the item with a credit purchase.

You are buying gas, checking into hotel, or renting a car.

Typically these type of vendors, determine the maximum amount you could spend and put a hold on your bank account for that amount to avoid being caught short on the transaction. For example, hotels protect themselves against incidentals and damages by adding an additional charge on your card. Generally, you can't access the frozen amount until the transaction is finalized (or you check out of your room and the access the charge), which can take up to 48 hours. You can always secure a hotel or car with a credit card then make the final purchase with debit.

You are looking to cash in on big rewards.

Credit cards historically offer better rewards on purchases than debit cards.

You can't check your account history often.

If do not frequently check your card history to monitor spending and fraudulent activity, you may want to consider using a credit card account. Legally if your credit card has been stolen, you are only liable for $50. However, debit transactions can sometimes leave you accountable for much more.

DON'T LET MEDICAL BILLS RUIN YOUR CREDIT

Medical bills are the leading cause of bankruptcy according to many financial sources. Unfortunately, many people neglect their medical bills without realizing the impact that those unpaid bills could have on their credit score.

How Medical Bills Can Harm Your Credit

After you receive medical services, your physician or hospital will bill you for any portion that wasn't covered by insurance. Just like any other bill, medical bills have a due date. If you don't pay by the due date, your bill becomes past due. Hospitals will only send you so many past due notices before they give your account to a third-party debt collector to resume collection efforts.

When the debt collector receives your medical bill, one of the first things it will do is report the account to one or all of the three major credit bureaus(Equifax, Experian and TransUnion). The medical collection account is considered a serious delinquency and can remain on your credit report for up to seven years, the maximum amount of time permitted by law.

Your credit score - the number creditors and lenders often use to approve your applications for new loans and credit - is based solely o information that's in your credit report. Since having a collection account on your credit report indicates you have a seriously delinquency in your credit history, your credit score will drop when a new collection is added to your credit report. The more medical collections accounts you have, the lawyer your credit score will be.

Protect Your Credit From Medical Bills

One of the easiest way to keep medical bills from impacting your credit score is to pay your bills when you receive them. If you can't afford to make payment in full, contact the hospital's billing department to make payment arrangements.

Even if you have health insurance, don't assume that your insurance company will always handle bills in a timely manner, If you receive a bill that should have been covered by insurance, contact your insurance company to find out why the bill wasn't paid. It could have been a simply oversight by hospital billing or the insurance claims department. Insurance companies often cover only a certain percentage of medical bills, So you might be responsible for some portion of medical debt after the insurance company has covered its part.

To be safe, contact the hospital or physician billing department to check the status of your account, especially if you've received any medical services within the past year. Just because the medical bill aren't on your credit report doesn't mean they don't exist. By contacting the medical provider, you'll be absolutely sure you don't have outstanding medical bills that could harm your credit.

DIVORCE & CREDIT

Divorce involves many complicated issues, such as support, alimony and property division. But who gets custody of your good credit?

Divorce can prove financially as well as emotionally stressful. If you find yourself faced with a divorce, it is important to start planning your financial future now. Follow these 10 guidelines to help maintain your good credit when going through a divorce :

- Know your current credit and debt situation. Obtain copies of your credit reports as well as your spouse's credit reports. Make a list off all debts and decide who is responsible for each account.
- Have a plan. Your divorce decree should state what will happen (frozen assets, wage garnishment, etc.) if your spouse stops making payments. Make sure you have quick legal resource if your spouse stops paying, and ensure your ability to make those payments yourself if necessary.
- Open a checking and saving account in your name only.
- Get at least one individual credit card and utility in your name only.
- Pay off all debts. Sell or refinance your house or other assets to cover outstanding debts, if necessary.
- Close joint accounts. Request that joint accounts be placed in the responsible party's name only as an individual account. If joint accounts cannot be reverted to individual accounts, then freeze joint accounts and tell the creditor that you will not be responsible for any more charges after that date.
- Remove all authorized users from your individual accounts - that especially means your spouse and his or her family members.
- Authorized users are not obligated to pay back any charges they make.
- Don't stop paying the bills. Keep making regular payments during the divorce process.
- Don't wait until you're in a crisis situation. Get you financial situation in order before you file for divorce.
- Contact your creditors. Your creditors are not a party to your divorce decree and are not legally bound by it. If your spouse fails to make a payment for a joint account, the creditor can and will pursue you for the money; it also will appear on your credit report. However, the creditor may enter into a separate payment arrangement with you or take your name off an account.
- Creditors are not required to change joint accounts to individual accounts. A creditor may require you to reapply for credit on an individual basis or refinance a mortgage in order to remove one spouse from the loan obligation.
- Get all agreements with creditors in writing. Make notes of all phone calls including names, dates and the topic of conversation. Don't have your name removed from any title if you are still responsible for the loan.
- Divorce is difficult even under the best of circumstances. Pay attention to credit issues before a divorce, and you can make the divorce process easier and relieve much of the stress.

DIVORCE & CREDIT

Who's Responsible For What?

Individual accounts: You are responsible for paying any debt in your name, whether you are married or not. If you live in a community property state, both you and your spouse may be responsible for debts incurred while married. Individual debt of one spouse may appear on both your credit report and your spouse's credit report.

Joint accounts: Both you and your spouse are responsible for paying the debt. This is true even if your divorce settlement states that one person will be responsible for the debt. Joint debts are reported to credit bureaus in both names.

Authorized users: You may authorize another person to use an individual account in your name, but you are responsible for the entire debt. If you are an authorized user on another person's account, you are not liable for the debt. However, the debt still may appear on your credit report.

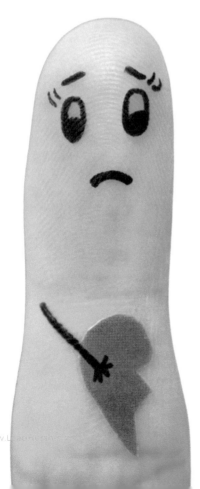
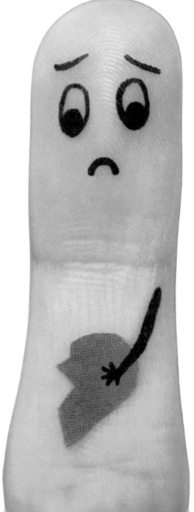

CREDIT BUILDING TIPS

Establishing a good credit history has never been as important as it is today.

It's not just that you'll need good credit to get decent rates when you're ready to buy a home or a car. Your credit history can determine whether you get a good job, a decent apartment, a deal on your cell phone and reasonable rates on insurance. One mirror misstep, a late payment, or spending over your credit limit can haunt you for years. If you're just starting out, you have a once-in-a-lifetime opportunity to build a credit history the right way. Here's what to do and what to avoid.

If age are previous credit troubles have prevented you from obtaining or re-establishing your credit, you may find it easier to obtain credit by applying for a gasoline card or a credit card with a department store.

You may also consider applying for a secured credit card. You will be a required to deposit a specified amount, usually $300 to $500 dollars into an account in their bank, and you will be issued a major credit card in the amount of the deposit. Shop around to find a bank that reports the card as an unsecured credit card on your credit file.

Take out a small loan from your credit union bank. Deposit the money into your savings account and pay the loan back monthly.

If you currently have credit, ask your creditors to increase your credit limit. This will improve your credit utilization ratio thereby improving your credit score. Just remember not to use the additional credit.

If you do not have a checking and saving account, apply for both. Having these accounts establishes you as part of the financial community and allows you to manage your money.

If a spouse or relatives has good credit, ask to be added as an authorized user to one or more if their accounts. This should never be done as a short-term fix to obtain a loan but should be used as a long-term strategy to help rebuild your credit. A word of caution: be very careful of whom you choose because if they make a late payment or default on a loan, it will appear on your credit report as well.

If you are faced with a financial crisis due to a job loss or unexpected medical bills, consider is asking a family member for a short-term loan to pay down your debt.

Your credit file also includes personal data such as your social security number, employment information, date of birth, and names and addresses you have listed when you applied for credit. Although this information is not used to calculate your credit score, it may be reviewed by banks and mortgage officers and used to make leading decision. Review your credit file for the following:

- Request that the credit bureau delete any social security numbers that are reporting in error.
- Make sure that your employment history is up to date and includes all positions you have held for the last five years.
- Make any necessary corrections, additions or deletions in regard to your current and previous addresses.
- Your credit score changes regularly as your creditors provide payment and account data to update your credit file. Your credit scores are always a reflection of your credit file at the moment in time the credit is pulled.

Atneciv Rodriguez

WAGE GARNISHMENTS

What is Wage Garnishment?

Wage Garnishment is a court-ordered repayment of an individual's debt through their employer. Under federal law, an employer must deduct a portion of an individual's pay in order to repay a creditor. The creditor must first obtain a court order to garnish that portion of the individual's earnings.

How is Wage Garnishment legal?

This law is administered by the Wage and Hour Division of the Department of Labor's Employment Standards Administration. Title III of the Consumer Credit Protection Act limits the amount of an employee's earnings which may be garnished and protects an employee from being fired if pay is garnished for one debt.

Which earnings can be garnished?

Under the law, any wage can be garnished, including hourly rates, salary rates, commission payments, bonuses, and retirement and pension incomes. Tips are not considered wages that can be garnished. The law applies in all 50 states, the District of Columbia, Puerto Rico, and all U.S. territories and possessions.

What is the maximum amount that can be garnished?

The amount of the garnishment, according to the law, either cannot exceed 25% of an individual's disposable earnings, which is a worker's take-home pay after federal, state, and local taxes, or the amount by which disposable earnings are greater than 30 times the federal minimum hourly wage, $5.15, which is $154.50. The creditor is allowed to garnish the lesser of the two. If the person makes more than $154.50 during a pay period, 25% can be garnished. Specific restrictions apply to court orders for child support or alimony. The garnishment law allows up to 50 percent of a worker's disposable earnings to be garnished if the worker is supporting another spouse or child, and up to 60 percent for a worker who is not. An additional 5 percent may be garnished for support payments more than 12 weeks in arrears.

What happens when Title III has been violated?

If an individual's rights under Title III have been violated by an employer, the individual must legally be reinstated at work and be paid back wages of the same amount that was wrongfully taken. If the employer does not abide by the laws, the individual may contact the Department of Labor, who will investigate the individual's case.

Are there any exceptions to the law?

The wage garnishment law specifies that garnishment restrictions do not apply to bankruptcy court orders and debts due for federal or state taxes. If a state wage garnishment law differs from the federal law, the law resulting in the smaller garnishment must be observed.

Where can I get more information?

For more information about the federal wage garnishment laws, you may contact the nearest office of the Wage and Hour Division, found under U.S. Government, Department of Labor, Employment Standards Administration.

FORECLOSURE

Understanding Foreclosure

Foreclosure isn't so much an event as it is a process--one that starts with you missing mortgage payments and ends with the lender taking your house and selling it. Timelines and specific procedures vary according to state laws, but the general outline is the same. Foreclosure doesn't happen overnight, and there are several points along the way at which you can stop the process and hold onto your home.

Missed Payments

Lenders typically begin formal foreclosure actions once you've missed three consecutive monthly payments. A missed mortgage payment is not the same as a late payment. A late payment is simply one that the lender receives after the due date, and most lenders even have a grace period of 10 to 15 days during which you can pay without penalty. A missed payment, on the other hand, is one that you don't make at all. Once a payment is 30 days late, it's missed. As you miss payments, you can expect to get letters and phone calls from your lender. Don't ignore them. At this point, it may be possible to work out a payment plan, but you have to communicate with your lender.

Notice of Default

After the third missed payment, you'll get a "notice of default" from your lender-- sometimes called a "demand letter" or a "notice to accelerate." This letter tells you how much you now owe, including interest, penalties and collection costs, and gives you a deadline to pay it, often within 30 days. You can stop the process right now by paying up or, if your lender is amenable, working out an alternative payment schedule.

Notice of Sale

When time runs out for you to pay up according to the default notice, the lender begins the actual foreclosure. Depending on your state law and the specifics of your home loan , the lender may have to get a court order allowing it to seize and sell the house, or it may already have that authority under a "power of sale" clause in the loan papers. Either way, once the lender has approval to foreclose, it schedules a date for your home to be auctioned off. You should receive a notice telling you when the sale date is, and a notice may also be posted on your door. By law, the sale usually has to be publicized, usually through an ad in a local newspaper.

Sale and Eviction

You may still be able to work out an arrangement with your lender up until the sale. If you can't, the home goes up for auction, and the highest bidder gets it. If no one bids on the house, or no one bids high enough, the home becomes the lender's property, referred to as an REO property, for "real estate-owned". The sale is the actual foreclosure. Once the sale occurs, you'll usually have some time to move out. If you don't, the sheriff will come and force you to leave.

Redemption

Most states allow you to halt the process at any time by paying off the mortgage in full, if you can somehow come up with the money. This is called "right of redemption." Sometimes the redemption period even extends past the date of the sale; if so, the notice of the sale will tell you how long you have to redeem the mortgage.

FORECLOSURE & SHORT SALE

Foreclosure and Short Sale: Which Option to Choose?

Losing your home to foreclosure as a result of not being able to keep up with your monthly mortgage payments can be one of the most devastating events you will ever experience. It is also an event that keeps on affecting you long after you lose your home because it destroys your credit score.

No one can be 100% sure that they will remain safe from foreclosure because they can't foresee the unexpected. Occurrences such as serious illness, a major accident, divorce or job loss can happen to anyone. With today's uncertain job market and economic climate, it's a good idea to understand the available alternatives should the worst occur.

Foreclosure is the worst of all available options

The inevitable result of a foreclosure is the lender taking your house. Not only will you lose your house, but the lender can get a judgment against you for any remaining balance you owe plus his costs for the foreclosure action. If that isn't enough, your credit report will be in terminal condition for many years to come, worsening an already bad financial situation and making it very difficult to obtain any other kind of credit. There is no upside to foreclosure. It should be avoided at all costs.

Consider a short sale when foreclosure seems inevitable

A short sale is a popular option for homeowners mired down with financial problems. In this case, you would sell your home for less than what you owe your lender; the biggest problem you will face is getting your lender to agree to a short sale. In many situations, they will not. Experts advise pursuing this option the minute you realize that you are falling behind in your payments and most likely won't be able to catch up. The longer you wait and the greater the amount you are in arrears, the less likely it becomes that your lender will even be willing to discuss a short sale.

A short sale has disadvantages too

While a short sale will save you from foreclosure, it will also have a negative effect on your credit score, frequently lowering it by as much as 200 points. This can be overcome more quickly than the devastation of a foreclosure, especially if you manage to retain one or two credit cards and keep them current. Perhaps equally distressing, the Internal Revenue Service frequently deemed the difference between the mortgage balance and the amount realized from the short sale to be taxable as income despite the fact that the debtor never saw a dime of it. Federal legislation called the Mortgage Forgiveness Debt Relief Act Of 2007 was designed to essentially eliminate this problem.

Almost any option is better than foreclosure

Simply stated, do everything you can before foreclosure occurs and do it as quickly as humanly possible. Don't sit back and keep thinking, "What can I do?" Instead, consider that short sale and check with your lender before your options become more limited.

Select a Skilled Realtor to Assist You

A successful short sale is dependent on a skilled real estate agent. Having someone who can work on your behalf is essential. Don't just get any real estate agent to help you! Select an agent with lots of short sale experience, he or she will know who to talk to, when to talk to them, and how to handle all the paperwork to get the deal done.

BENEFITS/DRAWBACKS
OF SHORT SALE

A short sale is when the lender agrees to accept less than the total amount owed on a real estate property. Though short sales do not protect your credit and you will see a drop in your credit score, a short sale may seem like a more favorable option than foreclosure for people that are in over their head.

Here are some reasons that a short sale may be the best option for you:

- You won't have to make any mortgage payments, unless you choose to.
- You can meet the new owners, rather than abandoning your home.
- Typically, credit will be restored in as little as 18 months.
- You may be able to obtain a mortgage quicker than if you were to foreclose on your home, sometimes within just a year or two.

Drawbacks of a Short Sale

- The lender may still require the difference of the sale price and the amount owed on the property to be paid. There is no guarantee that the lender will not legally pursue the balance.
- It may be hard to sell your property through the short sale process and you may end up foreclosing anyway. There is no assurance that the bank will accept the short sale offer on the property.
- The approval of the sale from the bank may be a long and frustrating process.
- The derogatory entry on your credit report can remain there for up to 7 years.

Be cautious: Some real estate agents recommend short sales because they get paid commission on the sale from the lender to do a short sale. When the bank takes back the property through foreclosure, the agent will not get paid.

How To Do A Short Sale

A short sale is a sale of real estate property where the lender agrees to accept less than the amount owed on the property's loan. Short sales are a way for homeowners to avoid foreclosure; however, 1) it does not always release the borrower from the obligation to pay the remaining balance of the loan to the lender and 2) a short sale will still negatively impact a credit report.

Short Sale Step-by-Step

How much is your property worth? Verify the value of your property either with a real estate broker or by comparing similar homes in the area.
Calculate the costs of selling the property, including all closing costs.
What do you owe on your property? This will be the total of all the loans against the property.
Determine the amount of the potential sale. Subtract total amount owing from the value of the property. If the number is negative, this means it will be a short sale.
Contact the lender to discuss your specific situation; if possible, talk to a supervisor or manager.
Discuss the procedures for a short sale with the lender, whether the lender reduces the amount owed or by making other arrangements. Some lenders believe that your debt is your responsibility and will not entertain other arrangements.

Almost any option is better than foreclosure
Simply stated, do everything you can before foreclosure occurs and do it as quickly as humanly possible. Don't sit back and keep thinking, "What can I do?" Instead, consider that short sale and check with your lender before your options become more limited.

JUDGEMENTS

Should you fail to pay your credit cards or other obligations, creditors will begin calling your house and workplace demanding payment. They will send you collection notices, threatening letters, and at some point, they may take you to court. If a judge decides that you are obligated to pay the debt, a judgment will be entered against you.

So what exactly is a judgment? A judgment is when a creditor files suit against you to demand payment for past-due obligations such as a charged-off credit card or personal loan. A judge hears the creditor's argument as to why you should pay the obligation, and then you are given the chance to present a counterargument as to why you should not be made to pay it. The judge then makes a decision. When a debt judgment has been entered, the judge has decided in the creditor's favor.

Going to court for a debt should be avoided at all costs, unless you are absolutely certain that you can win. It will affect your credit score and make you appear like a major credit risk to potential lenders, making it more difficult for you to obtain credit in the future. Additionally, a debt judgment is a public record, so when potential employers are conducting background checks on you, they will learn of the judgment against you.

You may win the case by arguing that the debt's statute of limitation has run out, or if it's not truly your debt, you can present documentation proving that. If you are not confident in your ability to win the case, contact the creditor directly and offer to pay a lump sum, or start making monthly payments in exchange for dropping the case. You may also ask the court to appoint a mediator to help resolve the situation without going before the judge to avoid a judgment.

Your initial inclination upon receiving a court summons may be to bury your head in the sand and hope the problem goes away on its own. It will not. If you fail to appear in court, the creditor wins by default. He can then petition the court to make you pay. At that point, the court can choose to garnish your wages until the debt is paid, or seize your assets to pay off the debt. On the other hand, if you show up to court and the creditor's representative does not, you win and the matter goes away.

BANKRUPTCY

What is bankruptcy?

Bankruptcy is a legal proceeding in which a person who cannot pay his or her bills can get relief from their debt. Bankruptcy allows individuals or businesses to either restructure their debt and pay it back within a payment plan, or have most of their debts absolved completely. Typically a bankruptcy filing stops all of your creditors from attempting to collect payments from you immediately or at least until your obligations are sorted out according to the law.

Why apply for bankruptcy?

When there are no other options available to you, filing for bankruptcy may give a much needed opportunity to gain control of your finances. For example, bankruptcy may make it possible to:

- Stop wage garnishments and harassing phone calls and letters from creditors.
- Legally relieve you from most or all of your debts.
- Prevent a foreclosure or repossession of your car and allow you to catch up on missed payments. Typically you will need to choose between continuing to make payments or giving the property back.
- Prevent you from having your utilities shut off.

How Will Bankruptcy Affect My Credit Score?

If you have seriously considered filing for bankruptcy, chances are your credit is already in poor shape. However, since bankruptcy either wipes out your old debts, or sets up a repayment plan, you will likely be in a better position to pay any current bills that you may owe. Bankruptcy will remain on your credit file for up to ten years, but you can begin to rebuild your credit history immediately by keeping your bills paid on time, not applying for excessive credit, and using only a small percentage of the credit limit available to you.

TYPES OF BANKRUPTCY

There are **four** different types of cases provided under the law:

- **Chapter 7** is commonly referred to as a straight bankruptcy or "liquidation". With the exception of taxes, student loans, or debts from fraud, embezzlement or larceny, a large part of your debt may be wiped out, but it's possible that some of your "non-exempt" property may be sold to help pay off your debts. The recent change in the bankruptcy law makes it harder to qualify for this type of bankruptcy, and it's likely that you will have to pay your auto loan and some of your old credit card debt. A Chapter 7 bankruptcy may be filed with a company as well, in this situation the business is forced to close, all assets of the company are sold, the creditors are paid with the proceeds.
- **Chapter 11** is used by businesses and is commonly known as "reorganization". Companies in serious financial trouble may be forced to file for bankruptcy protection with a federal bankruptcy court. Chapter 11 will allow the company to continue to operate while the court structures a repayment plan with the companies creditors. The court may relieve the company of all or part of its debt.
- **Chapter 12** is used by the farming community. This bankruptcy law was created to help family farmers keep their land, while reorganizing their debts through the bankruptcy court.
- **Chapter 13** allows an individual with a steady source of income to pay off bills and keep their property under a court approved repayment plan. This is also referred to as a "wage earner plan".

What Filing For Bankruptcy Cannot Do

- Bankruptcy cannot eliminate child support, alimony, most student loans, criminal fines, certain taxes or any debts that occur after the bankruptcy has been filed.
- Bankruptcy does not relieve any cosigners on your debts.
- Bankruptcy will also not eliminate any loans that were acquired with false information during the application process.
- Bankruptcy will not eliminate your mortgage or any other secured loan, it will only relieve you from other creditor payments so that you may catch up with your secured loans or house payment.

Alternatives To Bankruptcy

- The decision to file for bankruptcy has long term effects on the health of your credit and should be thought through very carefully. The following options may be considered as alternatives to bankruptcy:
- Consider finding additional income and cutting expenses. Many individuals have worked a second job in order to pay off credit card debt.
- Work directly with your creditors and make new payment arrangements.
- Get credit counseling to assist with planning and maintaining a budget.

Other Notes Regarding Bankruptcy
- Bankruptcy does not disqualify you for Social Security, Veterans Administration, Unemployment, or Welfare benefits.
- Recent changes in federal law require that within 180 days prior to the filing of a bankruptcy, you must participate in a budget and credit counseling course offered by an approved non-profit credit counseling agency.
- Bankruptcy will not resolve everyone's money problems, and there are many different reasons to file or not. If you are unsure, get legal advice.
- Public utilities cannot refuse or cut off service because you have filed for bankruptcy, however the utility can ask for a deposit for future service.
- A government agency or an employer cannot discriminate against you because you have filed for bankruptcy.

CHEXSYSTEMS

What Is ChexSystems?

ChexSystems is used by financial institutions to help assess the risk of opening a new checking or savings account for new customers.

If someone mishandled a checking or savings accounts in the past and still owes their old financial institution some money then they most likely have been reported to ChexSystems.

Unfortunately they probably won't know that until they try to open a new account somewhere and get declined. People are entitled to one free copy of a ChexSystems report per year, and the same goes with credit reports.

What is ChexSystems?

Just like a credit report records the way people handle their loans, credit cards, etc., ChexSystems records how they've handled their checking and savings accounts in the past. Unlike credit reports, they only record negative account information, the status of the accounts, and inquiries from other financial institutions. Information such as NSF activity, negative balances, outstanding debts, and account abuse are commonly reported items and will remain on the report for at least five years unless removed by the reporting source. This is just one of the ways the financial industry works together to keep people from burning multiple institutions.

How do Customers Get Out of ChexSystems?

After being reported and being denied to open accounts at all the local banks and credit unions it's easy to understand that options at this point are few and far between. It can be pretty hard to get one's finances in order if no financial institution is willing to open up an account. Some people will start cashing checks at a check cashing agency, paying bills with money orders, and borrowing money from payday loan centers. The fees from doing so will quickly cost far more money then what is owed to the previous financial institution that alerted ChexSystems.

So with that said, not only is it the right thing to do but the easiest and least expensive way to get out of the reporting system is to find the financial institution that filed the report in the first place and pay them back what is owed to them. Once they update ChexSystems or remove the negative info from the report that person should be free to once again open accounts at the financial institution of one's choosing.

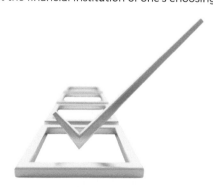

KEEPING SAFE

Access to public computers is convenient and a great resource for travelers and other consumers. Before you use the Internet, take time to understand the risks and learn how to spot potential problems. Enjoy the Internet with greater confidence, knowing you've taken the right steps to safeguard and protect your privacy while using a public computer.

Get savvy about Wi-Fi hotspots:

To protect your privacy, do not conduct personal transactions on Wi-Fi hotspots or public computers that request sensitive information such as bank account information, home address or your social security number. Wait to conduct these transactions on a private home computer.

Make Sure You Protect Your Personal Information

Delete your browsing history:
Simply use the browser tools available to delete your cookies and history when you are finished using a public computer. This will help to maintain your privacy and keep your information more secure.
Log out:
Anyone can access public computers. Close all browser tabs and log out of your accounts (some computers do this automatically but it is good to confirm). You wouldn't want just anyone to have access to your personal information and accounts.
Remember me "NOT":
Make sure the "remember me" function is not enabled on a public computer.

Use different passwords for every account.

Of course it's easier just to remember one password, but when has taking the easy route ever gotten you anywhere? When there is a large-scale password breech, as we saw with LinkedIn or Twitter, you can understand why having one password is the worst thing you can do. If the password and email address that you use for one account gets in the hands of the wrong person, they can start trying it on other sites and services. Make sure you use different passwords on different sites.

Make sure your passwords are strong.

You also have to make sure those passwords are good, hard-to-guess passwords. It is recommended that you use a mix of upper and lowercase letters and numbers and that you change your most important passwords at least once every six months and use password-manager software so you don't have to memorize them all.

Set up two-factor authentication.

Google recommends that two-factor authentication or two-step verification is something everyone should set up on his or her Google account. Other services provide similar security safeguards. When you sign into your account it requires you to enter another code, which you can only get via text or a phone call.

KEEPING SAFE

Protect your computer and browser.

This one used to be the most obvious and probably still is. Make sure if you are using a Windows PC you are using an up-to-date anti-virus or spyware program. Whether you are a Mac or a PC user, make sure your operating system is up-to-date with the latest security patches. Google also recommends using Chrome and making sure you have the latest version.

Secure your wireless connection.

Just as important is protecting the way you get onto the Internet. Make sure you have protected your home wireless network with a password and you have changed the default SSID, your network's name, from "Linksys" to something else. When connecting to public Wi-Fi networks be safe about what information you are sending over it.

Shop only at safe sites.

When making a purchase online, make sure the site has a little padlock icon next to the address and it has an HTTPS address before putting in your credit card number. If you are a frequent on line shopper, keep a close eye on your credit card bills for suspicious charges. In addition, make sure to look at the site and make an educated decision about its legitimacy. Google the site to see if any others have had issues with it.

Think before clicking links.

Clicking links is second nature on the Internet, but be careful before you click those lines of text. Anybody can create a template that looks like a bank and make it easy to click links and then access a computer or online account," experts say. Be vigilant about what links you click in an email, especially when they come from companies.

Protect your phone with a password.

Your phone is now a computer and can have as much or even more personal information than your laptop or desktop. Both experts firmly advised you password-protect smartphones. Android users should also consider security software or applications.

SAFE ONLINE SHOPPING

Online shopping is convenient, easy, and quick, but it's important to take steps to protect yourself. Before you start adding items to your cart, make sure you are up-to-date with the latest security software, web browsers and operating systems. Keeping your computer updated is the best defense against viruses, malware, and other online threats.

Tips to Keep Safe When Shopping

Check out sellers:

Conduct independent research before you buy from a seller you have never done business with. Some attackers try to trick you by creating malicious websites that appear legitimate, so you should verify the site before supplying any information. Locate and note phone numbers and physical addresses of vendors in case there is a problem with your transaction or your bill. Search for merchant reviews.

Make sure the site is legitimate:

Before you enter your personal and financial information to make an online transaction, look for signs that the site is secure. This includes a closed padlock on your web browser's address bar or a URL address that begins with http or https. This indicates that the purchase is encrypted or secured. Never use unsecured wireless networks to make an online purchase.

Use safe payment options:

Credit cards are generally the safest option because they allow buyers to request a refund from the issuer if the product isn't delivered or isn't what was ordered. Also, unlike debit cards, credit cards may have a limit on the monetary amount you will be responsible for paying if your information is stolen and used by someone else. Never send cash through the mail or use a money-wiring service because you'll have no recourse if something goes wrong. Don't forget to review return policies, you want a no-hassle ability to return items.

Keep a paper trail:

Print and save records of your online transactions, including the product description, price, online receipt, terms of the sale, and copies of any email exchange with the seller. Read your credit card statements as soon as you get them to make sure there aren't any unauthorized charges. If there is a discrepancy, call your bank and report it immediately.

Turn your computer off when you're finished shopping:

Many people leave their computers running and connected to the Internet all day and night. This gives scammers 24/7 access to your computer to install malware and commit cyber crimes. To be safe, turn off your computer when it's not in use.

Be wary of emails requesting information:

Attackers may attempt to gather information by sending emails requesting that you confirm purchase or account information. Legitimate businesses will not solicit this type of information through email. Contact the merchant directly if you are alerted to a problem. Use contact information found on your account statement, not in the email.

KEEP SAFE WITH SOCIAL NETWORKS

Facebook, Instagram, X, Threads, Twitter, Google+, YouTube, Pinterest, LinkedIn and other social networks have become an integral part of online lives. Social networks are a great way to stay connected with others, but you should be wary about how much personal information you post. To stay safe, read and follow these tips from StaySafeOnline – NCSA.

Have your family follow these tips to safely enjoy social networking:

Privacy and security settings exist for a reason: Learn about and use the privacy and security settings on social networks. They are there to help you control who sees what you post and manage your online experience in a positive way.

Once posted, always posted:

Protect your reputation on social networks. What you post online stays online. Think twice before posting pictures you wouldn't want your parents or future employers to see. Recent research found that 70% of job recruiters rejected candidates based on information they found online.

Your online reputation can be a good thing:

Recent research also found that recruiters respond to a strong, positive personal brand online. So show your smarts, thoughtfulness, and mastery of the environment.

Keep personal info personal:

Be cautious about how much personal information you provide on social networking sites. The more information you post, the easier it may be for a hacker or someone else to use that information to steal your identity, access your data, or commit other crimes such as stalking.

Know and manage your friends:

Social networks can be used for a variety of purposes. Some of the fun is creating a large pool of friends from many aspects of your life. That doesn't mean all friends are created equal. Use tools to manage the information you share with friends in different groups or even have multiple online pages. If you're trying to create a public persona as a blogger or expert, create an open profile or a "fan" page that encourages broad participation and limits personal information. Use your personal profile to keep your real friends (the ones you know trust) more synched up with your daily life.

Be honest if you're uncomfortable:

If a friend posts something about you that makes you uncomfortable or you think is inappropriate, let them know. Likewise, stay open-minded if a friend approaches you because something you've posted makes him or her uncomfortable. People have different tolerances for how much the world knows about them respect those differences.

KEEP SAFE WITH SOCIAL NETWORKS

Know what action to take:

If someone is harassing or threatening you, remove them from your friends list, block them, and report them to the site administrator.

Protect Yourself with these STOP. THINK. CONNECT. Tips:

Keep a clean machine:
Having the latest security software, web browser, and operating system are the best defenses against viruses, malware, and other online threats.

Own your online presence: When applicable, set the privacy and security settings on websites to your comfort level for information sharing. It's ok to limit how you share information.

Make passwords long and strong:
Combine capital and lowercase letters with numbers and symbols to create a more secure password.

Unique account, unique password:
Separate passwords for every account helps to thwart cybercriminals.

When in doubt, throw it out:
Links in email, tweets, posts, and online advertising are often the way cybercriminals compromise your computer. If it looks suspicious, even if you know the source, it's best to delete or if appropriate, mark as junk email.

Post only about others as you have them post about you.

PROTECTING YOUR PASSWORDS

Consider the number of personal identification numbers (PINs) and passwords, you use every day: getting money from the ATM or using your debit card in a store, logging on to your computer or email, signing in to an online bank account or shopping cart ... the list seems to just keep getting longer. Keeping track of all of the number, letter, and word combinations may be frustrating at times, and maybe you've wondered if all of the fuss is worth it. After all, what attacker cares about your personal email account, right? Or why would someone bother with your practically empty bank account when there are others with much more money? Often, an attack is not specifically about your account but about using the access to your information to launch a larger attack. And while having someone gain access to your personal email might not seem like much more than an inconvenience and threat to your privacy, think of the implications of an attacker gaining access to your social security number or your medical records.

One of the best ways to protect information or physical property is to ensure that only authorized people have access to it. Verifying that someone is the person they claim to be is the next step, and this authentication process is even more important, and more difficult, in the cyber world. Passwords are the most common means of authentication, but if you don't choose good passwords or keep them confidential, they're almost as ineffective as not having any password at all. Many systems and services have been successfully broken into due to the use of insecure and inadequate passwords, and some viruses and worms have exploited systems by guessing weak passwords.

How do you choose a good password?

Most people use passwords that are based on personal information and are easy to remember. However, that also makes it easier for an attacker to guess or "crack" them. Consider a four-digit PIN number. Is yours a combination of the month, day, or year of your birthday? Or the last four digits of your social security number? Or your address or phone number? Think about how easily it is to find this information out about somebody. What about your email password—is it a word that can be found in the dictionary? If so, it may be susceptible to "dictionary" attacks, which attempt to guess passwords based on words in the dictionary.

Don't assume that if you've developed a strong password you should use it for every system or program you log into. If an attacker does guess it, he would have access to all of your accounts. You should use these techniques to develop unique passwords for each of your accounts.

- Don't use passwords that are based on personal information that can be easily accessed or guessed.
- Don't use words that can be found in any dictionary of any language.
- Use both lowercase and capital letters.
- Use a combination of letters, numbers, and special characters.
- Use passphrases when you can.
- Use different passwords on different systems.

PROTECTING YOUR PASSWORDS

How can you protect your password?

Now that you've chosen a password that's difficult to guess, you have to make sure not to leave it someplace for people to find. Writing it down and leaving it in your desk, next to your computer, or, worse, taped to your computer, is just making it easy for someone who has physical access to your office. Don't tell anyone your passwords, and watch for attackers trying to trick you through phone calls or email messages requesting that you reveal your passwords.

Also, many programs offer the option of "remembering" your password, but these programs have varying degrees of security protecting that information. Some programs, such as email clients, store the information in clear text in a file on your computer. This means that anyone with access to your computer can discover all of your passwords and can gain access to your information. For this reason, always remember to log out when you are using a public computer (at the library, an internet cafe, or even a shared computer at your office).

"This information is provided for informational purposes only and does not represent an endorsement by or affiliation with the US-CERT (DHS), (a department of Homeland Security)."

IDENTITY THEFT

Identity theft involves acquiring key pieces of someone's identifying information, such as name, address, date of birth, social security number, etc., in order to impersonate them. This information enables the identity thief to commit numerous forms of fraud, which may include:

- Taking over the victim's financial accounts or obtaining fraudulent financial accounts;
- Making purchases in the victim's name;
- Applying for loans, credit cards, social security benefits, etc.;
- Establishing services with utility and phone companies.

What happens:

- Your credit could be destroyed.
- You may have to spend many hours on the phone and writing letters attempting to resolve the situation.
- You may experience difficulty in writing checks, obtaining loans, renting an apartment or buying a home.
- You receive bills and demands for payment for purchases that you never made.

Some Ways to Avoid Identity Theft or Lessen Its Consequences:

Empty your wallet or purse of extra credit cards or IDs (Social Security card, birth certificate, passport, etc.) - cancel cards you do not use. Memorize your Social Security number and any passwords/codes - do not record them on any cards or an anything in your wallet or purse. Shred pre-approved credit applications, receipts, bills and other financial information before discarding. "Opt out" of receiving pre-screened credit card offers by contacting the **Federal Trade Commission** (FTC) at 1-888-5-OPT-OUT or online at **www.optoutprescreen.com**.

Order a copy of your free credit report each year at **AnnualCreditReport.com**, the only authorized source for consumers to access their annual credit report online for free.

- Remove your name from mailing solicitation lists by writing to: The Direct Marketing Association, Mail Preference Service, PO Box 9008, Farmingdale, NY 11735-9008

- Remove your name from telephone solicitation lists by writing to: The Direct Marketing Association, Telephone Preference Service, PO Box 9014, Farmingdale, NY 11735-9014

- Remove your name from e-mail solicitation lists online by going to: The Direct Marketing Association

IDENTITY THEFT

Action Steps for Identity Theft Victims

Step 1

Contact your local law enforcement agency (and retain a copy of any filed report).

Step 2

Contact your credit card companies, banks, investment companies, licensing agencies, etc., by phone and in writing to inform them of the problem.

Step 3

Call your nearest U.S. Postal Inspection Service office (see federal government phone list)

Step 4

Call the three major credit agency Fraud Hotlines:

1. Equifax - 1-800-525-6285
2. Experian - 1-888-397-3742
3. TransUnion - 1-800-680-7289

Step 5

Call the Federal Trade Commission (FTC) Hotline to obtain its ID Theft Affidavit at 1-877-IDTHEFT.
- Or, send an electronic complaint to the FTC (The information you provide is up to you. However, if you do not provide your name or other information, it may be impossible for the FTC to refer, respond to, or investigate your complaint or request.)

Step 6

Contact the Social Security Adminstrations' Fraud Hotline at 1-800-269-0271.

Step 7

Keep a log of all your contacts and make copies of all documents.

IDENTITY THEFT

Be smart with your credit cards

- Reduce the number of credit cards you actively use and carry no more than two credit cards in your wallet or purse at a time.
- Cancel all unused accounts and cut up old credit cards before discarding.
- Report all lost or stolen credit cards immediately.
- Keep a list or photocopy of all of your credit cards, all account numbers, expiration dates and telephone numbers of customer service or fraud departments of your credit card companies and keep the list in a safe place not in your wallet or purse. (Do the same with all of your bank accounts.)Save all credit card receipts and match them to your monthly bills.
- Never give out your credit card numbers, bank account information or other personal information over the telephone, unless you have a trusted business relationship with the company and YOU have initiated the call.

Be smart with banks

- Always take your banking transaction receipts with you.
- Never toss receipts in a public trash can.
- Shred the receipts before disposal when you get home.
- Shred all old bank statements, cancelled checks and other banking records before disposal.
- Never give your PIN number or your ATM card to someone else.
- When ordering checks, keep personal information to a minimum.
- When ordering checks, either from your bank or from a check printing company, if the checks do not arrive in a timely manner (two to three weeks) notify your bank.
- Check your bank statements every month to make sure no one has accessed your account.

PREVENT PHISHING

There's a new type of Internet piracy called "phishing." It's pronounced "fishing," and that's exactly what these thieves are doing: "fishing" for your personal financial information. What they want are account numbers, passwords, Social Security numbers, and other confidential information that they can use to loot your checking account or run up bills on your credit cards. In the worst case, you could find yourself a victim of identity theft. With the sensitive information obtained from a successful phishing scam, these thieves can take out loans or obtain credit cards and even driver's licenses in your name. They can do damage to your financial history and personal reputation that can take years to unravel. But if you understand how phishing works and how to protect yourself, you can help stop this crime.

Here's how phishing works:

In a typical case, you'll receive an e-mail that appears to come from a reputable company that you recognize and do business with, such as your financial institution. In some cases, the e-mail may appear to come from a government agency, including one of the federal financial institution regulatory agencies.

The e-mail will probably warn you of a serious problem that requires your immediate attention. It may use phrases, such as "Immediate attention required," or "Please contact us immediately about your account." The e-mail will then encourage you to click on a button to go to the institution's Web site.

In a phishing scam, you could be redirected to a phony Web site that may look exactly like the real thing. Sometimes, in fact, it may be the company's actual Web site. In those cases, a pop-up window will quickly appear for the purpose of harvesting your financial information.

In either case, you may be asked to update your account information or to provide information for verification purposes: your Social Security number, your account number, your password, or the information you use to verify your identity when speaking to a real financial institution, such as your mother's maiden name or your place of birth.

If you provide the requested information, you may find yourself the victim of identity theft. How to protect yourself . . .

Never provide your personal information in response to an unsolicited request.

whether it is over the phone or over the Internet. E-mails and Internet pages created by phishers may look exactly like the real thing. They may even have a fake padlock icon that ordinarily is used to denote a secure site. If you did not initiate the communication, you should not provide any information.

If you believe the contact may be legitimate, contact the financial institution yourself.

You can find phone numbers and Web sites on the monthly statements you receive from your financial institution, or you can look the company up in a phone book or on the Internet. The key is that you should be the one to initiate the contact, using contact information that you have verified yourself.

FRAUD ALERTS

If you've been a victim of identity theft or want to prevent yourself from becoming one, you might be considering putting a security freeze on your credit file. While a freeze is in place, it greatly reduces the chance that anyone will be able to open credit in your name.

Requesting credit freezes at all three credit bureaus is a good idea if someone has actually stolen your identity. It is also worth considering if you suspect someone has stolen or otherwise obtained your Social Security number or other information that can be used to open credit in your name. But a security freeze may not be the best solution if the theft involves only your credit or debit card information, as with the recent data breaches at Target and Neiman Marcus.

First off, the primary danger from these breaches is that scammers may use your existing accounts to charge purchases or withdraw money. Neither of those actions requires accessing your credit file, which a security freeze is designed to prevent.

A freeze also has drawbacks. While it's in place, it prevents virtually everyone from accessing your credit files, even those you've authorized to do so (access still is permitted for companies with which you have existing relationships, such as your credit card issuers). That can create hassles, delays, and other problems if you need to apply for a loan, credit card, or a job; obtain insurance; rent an apartment; set up electric or phone service; and more. Most companies won't extend credit until they check your credit file at one or all of the three major credit bureaus. And some employers won't hire you without a credit check.

And unless you have a report from your police department or other agency indicating you're a victim of ID theft, it likely will cost you to set up, remove, or lift a security freeze at the three major credit bureaus. Fees range from $2 to $15 per bureau, depending on your state's laws.

When a Freeze is Necessary

If you're an actual victim of ID theft, a security freeze is a necessity. You should initiate one at all three major credit bureaus, Equifax, Experian, and TransUnion. You're likely entitled to a free freeze, though you may need to provide a report from a police or motor vehicles department, the Federal Trade Commission or some other agency. Check the bureaus' websites for more information about what you must do to initiate or lift freezes. Keep in mind that while the freeze is in place, virtually no one will be able to access your credit file, even those who may need to if you've applied for credit or a job.

WHEN YOU MIGHT CONSIDER A FREEZE

A freeze might be worth considering if you think you might become a victim of ID theft (you lost your wallet, for example), you're sure no one will need to access your credit file; or you live in a state that doesn't allow bureaus to charge a fees for freezes.

- Don't lose your PIN. If you do request a security freeze, don't lose the personal identification numbers the bureaus will provide you for use when lifting it. Some states allow bureaus to charge PIN replacement fees ranging from $5 to $10. (ID theft victims may be exempt from that fee as well.)
- Lift only one freeze if possible. If you need to lift a freeze, for example when setting up Internet service, find out if the company will tell you which credit bureau or bureaus it will use to check your file. If it's just one, you can save money by lifting the freeze only at that bureau instead of at all three.
- Consider a fraud alert. If you aren't a victim of ID theft but fear you could become one, an alternative is to place a free fraud alert on your credit file. When an alert is in place, your credit file will be accessible, but creditors must take reasonable steps to verify your identity before granting you credit. Unlike a credit freeze, which you must initiate at all three bureaus, you need only request a fraud alert at one. The request automatically will be sent to the others, typically within 48 hours. An initial alert lasts only 90 days. If you've been an actual victim of identity theft, you can request an extended alert, which lasts for seven years. During that period, a creditor must telephone you before it extends credit. To initiate an extended alert, you must provide an identity theft report from a police department or other agency.
- Change account numbers and check statements. Just because you chose any or all of these options doesn't mean you don't need to check your billing statements regularly, especially if a merchant informs you about a data breach that involves theft of your credit and debit card information. In these types of cases, it's vital to change the numbers of the affected accounts. Also monitor your billing and bank statements and report any unauthorized charges or debits immediately. And be on guard for anyone who may use the stolen card information in an attempt to trick you into revealing your Social Security number or other sensitive information, perhaps by contacting you by phone, email, or text and impersonating someone from a company you regularly do business with. As a further precaution, be sure to check your credit reports. Federal law entitles you to one free report from each of the three major credit bureaus every 12 months.

TEMPORARILY LIFTING A FREEZE

You can specify how long you want the freeze to be lifted — a day, week, or more. Temporarily lifting the freeze will allow you to apply with multiple lenders in order to get the best rate, as long as the applications are processed within the time frame you specified.

Allowing Only One Lender Access to Your Frozen Report

If you know for a fact that only one lender will be trying to access your report, you can choose to request a one-time-use PIN instead. Check with your lender in advance to make sure they have the ability to enter a single-use PIN when accessing your credit file. If they do, you can provide this PIN to the lender. This will allow only that particular lender to access your report a single time.

Permanently Removing Your Freeze

If you no longer wish to have a security freeze on your credit file, you can also request permanent removal online at the credit bureau's Freeze Center. You may also request removal by phone or by mail.

If you submit your request in writing, be sure to include the following information:

- Full name
- Complete address
- Social security number
- PIN
- Copy of a government issued identification card, such as a driver's license, state ID card, etc.
- Copy of a utility bill, bank or insurance statement, etc.

LIVING WITHOUT A CREDIT SCORE

How to Live Without Credit

Buying a Home

Don't have a credit score? Good. Despite what everyone says, you don't need one to buy a house! And if you've never gone into debt, that shouldn't be too difficult, right?

Now it's time to focus on one thing: making sure you have a large down payment to buy your next home. Without a credit score, your down payment is a big factor (along with your job and how long you've been employed in that line of work). You'll also want an outstanding history of rental and utility payments. Look for a mortgage company that uses a process called "manual underwriting," sometimes called "nontraditional credit" or "no credit score" lending.

If you're just starting your home-buying journey, be patient. Rent for a while if you need to and save up even more to put into a down payment. And whatever you do, don't buy a house until you're ready. That means you're completely out of debt, you have 3–6 months of expenses saved in an emergency fund, and you have a good down payment. Of course, if you really want to, you could always just pay straight cash for a house! Cash is king, baby!

Renting an Apartment

Most apartments will work with you if you can provide first and last month's rent, proof of being a good renter (such as previous on-time utility payments), and a security deposit. Be sure to ask them up front about their process and what type of information they'll need to get started.

If they want a credit score and you don't have one, simply tell them that you don't have debt and you use cash. Get a rental history referral from your previous landlord. If it's your first time renting, you might have to look around for a little bit. But don't worry, you'll be able to find someone to work with you.

Applying for a Job

This is a recent trend, but it mainly affects people in the financial industry—banks, mortgage brokers, investment companies and so on. Again, the key here is to learn the company's hiring process up front so you can explain why you don't have a credit score if they ask you about it.

Remember, these answers only apply if you have no credit score. If you have a bad credit score because of any outstanding debts, that's a different situation entirely. It's time to focus on cleaning up those old debts with the debt snowball method and start fresh!

Traveling

The naysayers out there want you to believe you can't travel without a credit card. But that's just not true! Your debit card (and cold, hard cash) works just as well—no, better—than a credit card. When you use your debit card, you're using money that you own and have worked hard for instead of borrowing on interest!

If you're looking into renting a room at a hotel, call ahead and let them know you'll be using your debit card. Then, make sure to budget for the possible security hold they'll put on your card for the duration of your trip.

You can also rent a car using your debit card. Companies like Dollar Car Rental have made it easier on people like you who live without a credit card! Like we said earlier, just call ahead and ask about any holds they might place on your debit card and budget for your trip accordingly.

LIVING WITHOUT A CREDIT SCORE

Benefits of Living Without Credit

It's time to measure your success (and financial worth) in a different way—by what's in your bank account. Who said the credit score is the only way things can be done?Now that we know you can buy and rent a car, take out a mortgage, and even get a hotel room without a credit score, let's dive into some other reasons living without credit cards is a great idea:

1. **You're no longer enslaved to a life of debt.** When you're not enslaved to your credit score (or your credit cards for that matter), you're no longer worried about payments for things you've purchased in the past—or worried about how you're going to pay for your future. Not only that, you're also free. You're free to spend your money on the present and save for the future.

2. **Your bank account becomes your measuring tool**. If you haven't heard, the FICO score is just another name for the "I love debt" score. Think about it: Businesses, banks and even the government use this silly little number to analyze your past and present relationship with debt. But when you choose to leave all care about your score behind, you get to measure things by what you actually have in your bank account (and what you can afford).

3. **You're in complete control of your finances.** Like we've said before: Cash is king, baby! When you start saving up for life's big purchases (to pay in cash), you'll find that a credit score is worthless. Not only will you have the power of negotiation on your side, but you'll also find out how much easier it is to buy things outright. Who's going to turn down cash?

4. **You're less likely to overspend.** When you're not relying on a credit card for "emergencies," you have one option: to pay for things with the money you have in your bank account. When your money is gone (or spoken for with your zero-based budget), you're done spending. Living life without credit means you know exactly what it's like to live within your means—and it feels good.

5. **You'll build wealth and give generously.** When you're debt-free and you've reached a Step where it's all about building wealth and giving. Yup, that dream retirement you and your spouse have been working so hard for is finally at your fingertips. Maybe you've always wanted to travel overseas to help a nonprofit organization or give 50% of your earnings to charity every year. The options are endless, because you're not tied to making payments every single month. Instead, you get to dream of what it can be like to use your wealth to help others. And that feels good.

You Can Live Without a Credit Score!

Our culture will tell you otherwise, but living without credit is possible! Sure, sometimes it might feel a little inconvenient because of the way our culture has embraced the "almighty" FICO. But seriously, living without a credit score will never be as inconvenient as paying interest on that fancy steak dinner you ate . . . last year.

Are you ready to break up with your credit score yet? Learn how to dump debt, save for emergencies, and build a solid financial future—plus get all the tools you need to make it happen. Why? Because FICO doesn't determine your worth. You do.

WHAT IS THE ENVELOPE SYSTEM?

The envelope system is a way to track exactly how much money you have in each budget category for the month by keeping your cash tucked away in envelopes created by financial guru Dave Ramsey. At the end of the month, you can see how much cash is left by taking a quick peek in your envelope. How easy is that?

If you're constantly going overboard in a certain category (hello, food!), then take cash out for the amount you've budgeted for and stick it in an envelope. When you shop for that category, only use what's in the envelope. Once the money is gone, it's gone—so this will force you to stop overspending!

How the Envelope System Works

One of the reasons we overspend is because there's nothing telling us when to stop. That's where your cash envelopes come in. They work as a great tool to help you stick to your budget. Here's how to use them:

1. Think of the budget categories that need a cash envelope. It's a good idea to use the envelope system for items that tend to bust your budget. Think of things like groceries, restaurants, entertainment, gas and clothing.

You get to decide which budget categories get an envelope, but here are a few I find most helpful:
- Groceries
- Restaurants
- Gas
- Medicine/pharmacy
- Hair care/makeup
- Car maintenance
- PersonalEntertainment
- Gifts

2. Figure out your budget amount. If you know you tend to overspend on things like baby showers, birthdays and impulse buys, then look at limiting that to a certain amount for the month. If groceries are always zapping your cash, figure out how much you want to spend on them and then stick to it!

Make sure you and your spouse are on the same page with the budget amounts. And if you're single, recruit an accountability partner who is committed to holding you to your budget. This could be a friend, family member or coworker who you trust and know is on board with the money principles you're putting into practice.

WHAT IS THE ENVELOPE SYSTEM?

3. Create and fill cash envelopes for the budget categories. Let's say you've budgeted $500 a month for groceries. When you get your first paycheck of the month, take out $250 from your bank account and put the cash in an envelope. On that envelope, write out Groceries. When you get your second paycheck, do the same thing again and put that $250 in the envelope. That's your $500 food budget for the month.

Make sure you take enough money with you to cover your groceries for that trip. If you take $150 cash and your total comes to $160, take some things out of the cart and put them back. I know, I know—it's hard! But it's better than going over on your grocery category and busting your whole budget for the month!

And on the flip side, if you don't spend all of the money from the groceries envelope when you're at the store, make sure you put any change you get back in the cash envelope.

No money—and I mean zero money—comes out of that groceries envelope except to pay for food at the grocery store. If you go food shopping and leave the envelope at home by mistake, turn your car back around!

4. Spend only what you've put in each cash envelope. Don't forget: When your money's gone, it's gone! If you want to go to the store but don't have enough money, raid the fridge for leftovers. Do a pantry challenge! Dig through your pantry to see what you can find to make dinner without having to hit the grocery store. This is a great way to really get intentional about your spending habits!

Advantages to Using Cash Envelopes
- It keeps you on track.
- It enforces discipline.
- It holds you accountable.
- It makes it pretty hard to overspend.

What If I Pay Some of My Expenses Online?

Here's the thing with the envelope system: It works better when you're actually physically walking into a store to make a purchase. Shopping at the grocery store, going out to eat, getting a haircut or oil change are all times when using the envelope system works really well!

You can still use cash envelopes for online purchases, but it does get a little trickier. Write the amount you've budgeted for on the outside of the envelope and don't spend more online than the amount you've jotted down. Keep track of how much you've spent and write it on the back of the envelope, just like if you were balancing a checkbook.

WHAT IS THE ENVELOPE SYSTEM?

What If I Run Out of Money in My Cash Envelope?

Be careful not to borrow from the other cash envelopes. When it comes to the envelope system, it can be really tempting to shuffle cash from one category to fund another.

Let's say you used up all the money in your restaurants envelope—don't be surprised if some inner voice tells you to grab your clothing envelope.

Remember, the whole purpose of using cash envelopes is to control your spending and help you stick to your budget.If you run out of restaurant money, eat leftovers instead of going out. If you see your gas money slipping away faster than you planned, limit your trips or start carpooling to work. Find creative ways to make your money stretch when the envelopes are getting low!

What About Emergencies?

If you have a crisis come up in the middle of the month or something happens and you have absolutely no choice but to shift your envelope funds, call an emergency budget meeting to talk it through.

If you're married, talk with your spouse and figure out the best course of action, adjust the budget, and agree on it together. Both of you must be involved—it's a joint decision. Or if you're single, run the amounts by your accountability partner to get their input.

What If I Have Money Left at the End of the Month?

If you have money left in an envelope at the end of the month, congratulations! You came in under budget! That's the best feeling in the world. And it's okay to celebrate too . . . within reason.

Reward yourself by going out to dinner or grabbing a pumpkin spiced latte. Or roll the money over to next month so you have an extra-large food budget. Rewarding yourself is important because it helps keep you motivated. You have to celebrate those little wins along the way!

And if you're in Baby Step 2, take that extra cash and put it toward your debt snowball. Every little bit helps!

Remember, cash envelopes are powerful weapons in the fight against overspending. They can help you manage your money better than you ever have. Put the Ramsey envelope system to work for you and get intentional about how you're spending your money!

ROADMAP TO SUCCESS

Once you complete the task, check the box to show your progress

MONTH 1

Begin Credit Restoration, Send dispute letters - www.Leadhership.biz

Begin Credit Monitoring, monitor your credit activity, and watch for alerts regarding changes in your credit.

Set up identity theft monitoring and know your personal information is protected.

MONTHS 2-3
Build your credit score

Apply for a secure credit card to add positive tradelines to your credit report. www.leadhership.biz

Report your rent payments to the bureaus by enrolling in our Credit My Rent Program
www.leadhership.biz

Utilize the Credit Builder tool to provide you with information on how your credit score is calculated and tips on improving your results

MONTHS 4-6
Work on any outstanding debt

Activate membership to get access to services and information.

Pay off your debt faster with our improved Debt Payoff system

Track your income and spending by setting up your monthly budgeting program.

MONTHS 7-9
Establish your family's security

Create your Will, Trust, Medical, and financial POA to protect your family assets

Protect and secure your financial documents in our Financial Tool Kit

Develop your savings goals and plan for future expenses such as college tuition or that special vacation

MONTHS 10+
Stay on top of your finances

If you are experiencing debt harassment or need legal help with credit reporting errors, contact our Credit Staff to assist you

Calculate your Net Worth and manage your family's assets and liabilities

Enroll your children in the Youth financial literacy program. This program is full of powerful financial information for the youth of America

LETTER TO NEGOTIATE A COMPLETE REMOVAL WITH A CREDITOR

Date

Original creditor (or name of collection agency if the account was sold)
Creditor address
City, state, Zip

RE: (Bank of America - account #) (if contacting a collection agency include the original account number, i.e., the Visa number in this case, and also include any account number assigned by the collection agency –this number would be on one of your collection letters)

Dear Customer Relations Manager: (If you are contacting the original creditor. If you are contacting a collection agency, use - To Whom It May Concern)

After recently reviewing my credit report, I discovered that the above-mentioned account is currently in (charge off/collection) status. I would like to resolve the payment on this account as soon as possible.

Due to [whatever caused you to be late on your payments, ex: illness], I, unfortunately, became behind on my payments and was unable to meet my obligations. However, since then my situation has greatly improved and I am in the position to pay this debt.

I am willing to pay [creditor's name] [x payments a month] equaling the amount of [total they are requesting] provided that the above account is updated on all credit reporting agencies to state "PAID AS AGREED", or removed entirely from all credit reporting agencies upon my final payment.

I am not agreeing to an updated credit report that states this account as: "PAID CHARGE OFF" or the like, as this will not significantly increase my credit score, nor will it reflect my sincere willingness to restore my good name and hopefully, someday, again do business with your company.

I am hoping for your written response agreeing to the agreement to my proposal and upon receipt, I will begin payments. Thank you very much for your valuable time.

Best regards,
 [first & last name] [street address] [city, state, zip code]

LATE PAYMENT REMOVAL REQUEST LETTER (GOODWILL)

Everyone knows that recent late payments can be challenging to remove from your credit file. This letter has been designed to request a goodwill removal and can be tailored to address your own unique situation.

[your full name]
[your full address]
[your full phone number]
Dear Customer Relations:

This letter is in reference to a late payment with the account number [xxxx].

Last year due to extreme financial hardship and medical problems, I became seriously behind on several of my bills. While I normally make a great effort to honor my debts and fulfill my responsibilities, at the time of the late payments I was simply financially not able to pay my bills.

I have since gotten back on my feet and brought my account up to date with your company.
I am now trying to buy a home, however, I am having difficulties receiving an affordable rate due to the impact of having a late payment on my credit file. I am hoping that your organization will consider removing this late payment from my credit report as a gesture of goodwill. This kind gesture would sincerely be appreciated and an invaluable gift to my family and me.

Sincerely,

Your Signature

SAMPLE CEASE AND DESIST LETTER FOR DEBT COLLECTORS

You can use this cease and desist letter to stop debt collectors from calling you. Once the collector receives your letter, the FDPCA allows the collector to contact you one final time, in writing, to let you know what action, if any, the collector will take next.

Date

Your Name
Address
City, State Zip

Debt Collector's Name
Address
City, State Zip

Re: Account Number

Dear Debt Collector:
Pursuant to my rights under federal debt collection laws, I am requesting that you cease and desist communication with me, as well as my family and friends, in relation to this and all other alleged debts you claim I owe.

You are hereby notified that if you do not comply with this request, I will immediately file a complaint with the Federal Trade Commission and the [your state here] Attorney General's office. Civil and criminal claims will be pursued.

Sincerely,

Your Name

SETTLEMENT LETTER
OFFER TO PAY IN EXCHANGE FOR
DELETE OF ACCOUNT

A pay-for-delete agreement is where you agree to pay off your debt in full or negotiate to settle your debt with the creditor/collection agency in return of their promise to erase all information on this account from your credit report. You'll need to prepare and send a letter such as this to get a response in writing. Here is a sample that can be tailored to your individual needs:

Your Name
 Your Address
City, State, Zip
 Your Phone#

Creditor/Collector's Name
 Creditor/Collector's Address
City, State Zip

Date

 Dear Creditor/Collection Manager,

Re: Account Number_____

This letter is in response to your (select one) call/letter/credit report entry on [date] for the collection account listed above. I would like to (pay off) or (settle this debt in full).

As of today, this debt has not been verified. This letter does not imply a promise to pay the debt unless you provide a response as requested below.

I am aware of the fact that your company can report the debt to the credit bureaus as you find necessary. Moreover, you have the ability to change the account status since you are the information provider.

I am willing to offer $_____ as payment or settlement of the debt in full in return of your agreement to remove all information on this account from my credit report within 10 calendar days. If you agree to the terms, I shall send you a certified payment of the amount stated above in exchange for having all information on this debt account deleted from my credit report.

I am also requesting that you provide this information to the original creditor, if applicable. If you find my offer acceptable, please send me a letter agreeing to the terms. The letter should be subject to the laws of my state and treated as a contract.

As per the Fair Debt Collection Practices Act, I have the right to dispute this alleged debt. In case I do not receive your postmarked response within the next 15 days, I shall withdraw the offer and request full verification of this debt.

I look forward to hearing favorably from you.

Sincerely,

Signature
Your Name

Your Name

RESOURCES

Report Credit Repair Fraud

State Attorneys General

Many states also have laws regulating credit repair companies. If you have a problem with a credit repair company, report it to your local consumer affairs office or to your state attorney general (AG).

Federal Trade Commission

You also can file a complaint with the Federal Trade Commission. Although the FTC can't resolve individual credit disputes, it can take action against a company if there's a pattern of possible law violations. File your complaint online at ftc.gov/complaint or call 1-877-FTC-HELP.

Federal Trade Commission Consumer Infor
https://www.consumer.ftc.gov/

Consumer Financial Protection Bureau
https://www.consumerfinance.gov/consumer-tools/credit-reports-and-scores/

Free Credit Reports
http://www.annualcreditreport.com/
call 1-877-322-8228

Credit report request form
https://www.consumer.ftc.gov/sites/www.consumer.ftc.gov/files/articles/pdf/pdf-0093-annual-report-request-form.pdf
mail it to:
Annual Credit Report Request Service,
P.O. Box 105281,
Atlanta, GA 30348-5281

Equifax: 1-800-685-1111; equifax.com

Experian: 1-888-397-3742; experian.com

TransUnion: 1-800-916-8800; transunion.com

NOTES

/ /

S M T W T F S

BUDGET PLANNER

MONTH:_____

INCOME STREAMS

AFTER TAX	BUDGET	ACTUAL	DIFFERENCES
Income			
Side Hustles			
Business			
Others			

FIXED AND VARIABLE EXPENSES

EXPENSES	BUDGET	ACTUAL	DIFFERENCES

SAVINGS

	TOTAL SAVINGS
Total Income (After Tax)	
Total Fixed Expenses	
Total Variable Expenses	
Savings - Income + Expenses	

NOTES

/ /

S M T W T F S

EXPENSE TRACKER

MONTH OF

DATE	DESCRIPTION	CATEGORY	AMOUNT
			TOTAL

NOTES

/ /   S M T W T F S

FINANCIAL GOALS

My Goal:

Starting Balance:

Per Day:

Per Month:

Required Amount

Due Date

Notes

DEBT TRACKER

Creditor

DEBT TYPE	STARTING BALANCE	CREDIT LIMIT	ACCOUNT NO.

INTEREST RATE	MIN REPAYMENTS	REPAYMENT FREQ	PAY OFF BY

DATE	REPAYMENT	BALANCE	NOTES

ANNUAL BILLS

YEAR _____

DUE DATE	EXPENSE	AMOUNT	J	F	M	M	A	J	J	A	S	O	N	D
		TOTAL												

QUARTERLY BILLS

JAN - MAR / APR - JUNE / JUL - SEP / OCT - DEC

DUE DATE	BILL	AMOUNT	PAID
		TOTAL	

EXECUTIVE LEADERSHIP LLC

SCAN ME!
TO VIEW OUR SITE

CHECK OUR SITE ONLINE, OPEN YOUR
PHONE CAMERA AND SCAN THIS QR CODE

PHONE NUMBER:
1203-805-8575

WWW.LEADHERSHIP.BIZ

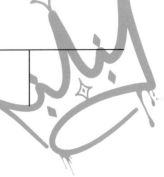

ABOUT THE AUTHOR

Hey!

I'M ATNECIV RODRIGUEZ

Atneciv Rodriguez, MBA, A serial entrepreneur whose passion is to help other entrepreneurs build, grow and sustain in Business, Finances, and Mindset. She empowers her readers to trust their intuition and create their own opportunities and fulfill whatever their desires are.

With her system of Business and finances, she has helped hundreds of people especially women bring their passions to life and held them accountable to put their ideas into action.

Atneciv has been professionally certified and licensed in Life Coaching, Business Consulting, Financial Literacy, Credit, Insurance, Taxes, Investments, and in Esthetics for her other businesses.

For more information visit
www.LeadHership.biz
info@leadhership.biz